MODERN
Faux Flower
PROJECTS

Faux flower arrangements
can be just as stunning as
fresh flowers.

MODERN Faux Flower PROJECTS

Fresh, Stylish Arrangements and Home Décor with Silk Florals and Faux Greenery

STEVIE STORCK

Photography by Savannah Smith

FOX CHAPEL
PUBLISHING

ISBN 978-1-4971- 0047-3

Names: Storck, Stevie, author.
Title: Modern faux flower projects / Stevie Storck.
Description: Mount Joy : Fox Chapel Publishing, [2019] | Includes index. |
  Summary: "Contains information on choosing and arranging faux flowers
  through various methods. Also includes step-by-step instructions on
  creating twelve faux floral arrangements inspired by the four seasons"--
  Provided by publisher.
Identifiers: LCCN 2019033529 (print) | LCCN 2019033530 (ebook) | ISBN
  9781497100473 (paperback) | ISBN 9781607657194 (ebook)
Subjects: LCSH: Flower arrangement. | Artificial flowers.
Classification: LCC SB449.3.A7 S76 2019 (print) | LCC SB449.3.A7 (ebook)
  | DDC 745.92--dc23
LC record available at https://lccn.loc.gov/2019033529
LC ebook record available at https://lccn.loc.gov/2019033530

To learn more about the other great books from Fox Chapel Publishing, or to find a retailer near you, call toll-free 800-457-9112 or visit us at *www.FoxChapelPublishing.com.*

We are always looking for talented authors. To submit an idea, please send a brief inquiry to acquisitions@foxchapelpublishing.com.

Printed in China
First printing

"Floral design is an art form: the flowers are your tools and you are the artist."

—*Alyssa Grogan of The Rogue Petal Co., Baltimore, MD*

There are so many ways to capture your home's aesthetic with faux flowers, and this book can be used as a source of inspiration for you. See page 114 to see how I made this colorful project.

Contents

Introduction

FAKE FLOWERS, REAL BEAUTY

It's no secret that artificial flowers and plants have a little bit of an image problem. The word "faux" lends a touch more class, but the commonly used descriptor "fake" has a rather negative connotation. As an amateur gardener and generally floral-obsessed person, there's not much I love more than a bouquet of fresh flowers or a happy houseplant. But as a crafter and decorator (I'm an interior designer by trade), I know faux has an important role. It's not an either/or decision between artificial and fresh, it's an AND. In this book, I share DIY tips and inspiration for creating beautiful faux floral arrangements and projects for decorating your home seasonally, for special occasions, and for every day.

To keep your faux flower arrangements looking contemporary, seek out current floral designs for inspiration.

Artificial flowers and plants are experiencing a renaissance in the home décor world, and it's not hard to see why! They have many great things going for them. Never before have artificial flowers been more realistic or more widely available. Take one visit to your nearest craft store and you'll see just about every type of faux florals, greenery, and supplies. More and more big box stores and specialty online shops are popping up to meet the demand. Faux florals are a long-lasting and low-maintenance alternative to fresh-cut flowers and live plants. Faux saves money over time compared to continuously replenishing fresh and live plants. And lastly, there are things you can do with faux plants that just aren't as easy with fresh ones. You can make an arrangement as a centerpiece for your holiday table, reuse it again the following year, or pull it apart and rework the florals into a beautiful wreath for your front door. Fresh just doesn't have the same versatility. I argue that if you're going to take the time to handcraft something, why wouldn't you want it to stick around for more than a couple of days?

If you've picked up this book, I'm guessing you already know these things and have an interest in crafting with artificial flowers. Or perhaps you are just curious as to how faux flowers could possibly be modern and stylish when you've always thought of them as old-fashioned and outdated. It's not the flowers that are outdated—it's the inspiration. Instead of looking to what's been done with faux flowers before, we should be looking to the work of contemporary fresh floral designers and the beauty of nature for inspiration. High-quality faux florals have become so lifelike that some are nearly indistinguishable from fresh. It's time that the world of artificial flowers got some fresh ideas. That's what I hope to provide through this book! Inspiration for you to design and create your own artificial flower projects. The only limit is your imagination.

Found items, like this birdcage, can always be upcycled into a beautiful décor item for your home.

Create pieces to fit your home rather than trying to fit handmade pieces into your décor.

MY CRAFTING MANIFESTO

First of all, let me be clear: I am not a professional florist. I am an interior designer, blogger, wife, and mother who enjoys crafting in my spare time. I have no formal training in floristry. I would describe myself as a self-taught hobbyist and general flower enthusiast. Hopefully, that gives you some confidence: You don't have to be a pro to craft beautiful faux flower projects for your home. If I can do it, then so can you!

As I've gotten older, I've become less interested in crafting as a form of entertainment and more interested in crafting things that I would actually want to display in my home. Like me, I bet you have made something, and then tried to find a spot for it. Instead, find a spot in your home that needs decorating, and then make something to fit that space. When it comes to interior design and homemaking, I ascribe to what I call "Essentialism." In home decorating terms, that means spaces that feel peaceful, uncluttered, and easy to live in. Instead of being a minimalist or maximalist, I believe in outfitting rooms with just enough furnishings and décor to feel full, while still allowing for room to grow as you live life in your home. Simple, classic, and timeless is the goal.

I believe that a well-designed home is one that tells the story of the people who live in it. To me, that means using meaningful pieces, such as family heirlooms or objects you've collected through your travels, as a part of your everyday décor. Making your own handcrafted décor is an excellent way to personalize your home design with one-of-a-kind items that express your unique style.

My personal style is all about elevating simplicity and infusing meaning into our lives at home. My craft projects might not be the most flashy or intricate, but I design them with thought and care. Whether the design is based around a memory from my childhood, a found object I want to repurpose, a place that has captured my heart, or just a color scheme I love, I try to infuse meaning into everything I create. I hope you'll enjoy reading about the inspiration behind the 12 projects in the second half of this book and take that as an invitation to use your own creativity and experiences to inform the way you craft and decorate.

Personalize your home with handmade, unique items.

My love of flowers and the knowledge I've gained as an interior designer come together in this book. I wanted to show people how beautiful and wonderful faux flowers can be.

PART I:
GETTING STARTED

Decorating with faux flowers and plants gives you the freedom to create any arrangement, in any type of vessel, anywhere in your house, with no worries about water or sunlight.

CHAPTER 1: FAUX FLORALS 101

Before we get into how to design and craft with artificial flowers and greenery, let's first talk a little bit about what they are and how they are made. You might be surprised to learn that permanent botanicals have been around for centuries! As far back as Ancient Egypt, people have been imitating natural flowers with a wide variety of materials, including linen, shavings from animal horn, seashells, wax, gold, and silver. It was in Italy in the twelfth century that flowers began to be made from silk. Although artificial florals are still commonly referred to as "silk," these days most are made from polyester and plastic: polyester fabric for the flower petals and leaves, and plastic for the stems, berries, and smaller plant parts such as pistils and stamens. Flower petals are made by cutting thin layers of polyester fabric and then pressing them in heated molds, which add shape and texture. They are assembled and colored using a variety of methods. Sometimes stacks of polyester flower petals are painted by hand with watercolors; sometimes they are silk-screened to create specific patterns; and sometimes they are dipped in clear or pigmented polymer that makes petals and leaves feel more realistic to the touch.

There are three main types of faux floral products you can buy: stems, sprays, and bushes. Stems are single flowers on a longer stem. Often a stem will also have leaves, and sometimes it will have a small bud as well. Sprays will have multiple flower heads, leaves, or buds on a longer stem. Bushes usually have many shorter stems of flowers or leaves that are joined at the base. Bushes can be used as-is or cut down into pieces to use in arrangements. A hanging bush will have a long cascade of flowers or leaves that are joined at the base with a thicker stem. These can be used in taller flower arrangements or on their own in a hanging planter for a pretty trailing look. Flowering branches can be used as another faux floral component to an arrangement. Craft stores will also typically sell artificial flowers in premade bundles or bouquets, swags, and garlands.

Types of faux floral products, from left to right: stem, spray, and bush.

Although modern faux flowers are still sometimes referred to as "silk," they're mostly made from plastic and polyester.

"Quality is important. You should choose high- quality materials, from the flowers to the foam to the cutting tools. Cutting corners typically leads to frustration and will take the enjoyment out of it for you!"

—Stephanie Kirby of The Blue Daisy Floral Designs, Pittsburgh, PA

How to Choose Flowers

With all the options available, it can be hard to find a place to start when shopping for faux flowers and greenery. Here are a few methods I use that I hope will be helpful in planning your next faux floral craft project.

Quality/Realism

Faux florals and greenery come in a wide variety of types and quality levels. My advice is to choose the best-quality flowers you can afford. If you invest in better-made florals and supplies, not only will your finished project look more realistic, but it will also last longer. Although there is a plethora of artificial flowers out there in every color you can imagine, I recommend sticking to options that mimic nature as much as possible. You can find a bush of cobalt blue daisies at the craft store, but maybe go for the simple white and yellow option instead.

Craft stores will often have several styles and colorways of the same flower type available. Even slight differences can make a flower look truer to life. For example, in the spring tabletop arrangement (see page 96), I chose cream tulips instead of white because the cream had more dimension and color variation. That made them look more like a real tulip to me, whereas the stark white felt a little more faux.

Season

Choose flowers that are in bloom in the same season for a great way to keep your faux arrangement feeling natural and cohesive. In spring, you could make an arrangement of tulips, daffodils, and dogwood branches. In summer, you could use poppies, cosmos, and daisies. In fall, think about goldenrod, chrysanthemum, and rust-colored leaves. Finally, in winter, mixing evergreen branches and berries into your arrangement gives a seasonal feel. That said, the benefit to faux is that you can bend the rules a bit! Peonies generally bloom in the late spring, but who's to say you can't feature a beautiful burgundy peony in a fall arrangement? Use this method as a means of inspiration, but don't limit yourself.

Color

Having a color scheme in mind is a great way to shop for faux flowers. Are you looking for a minimal, monochromatic color palette for your arrangement? Maybe you want something bold and high contrast with purples and yellows? Many craft stores arrange their floral department by color, which makes it easy to build your arrangement as you shop. See page 74 for more on choosing a color scheme for your arrangement, along with some example color schemes that I love.

Choosing faux flowers that match the real flowers that are currently blooming will ensure that your décor keeps up with the seasons.

Buying faux florals will be easier if you have a color scheme in mind before shopping.

TIP

Pare down the color scheme if you want a wide variety of flowers. If you want a lot of color, keep it simple with just a few kinds of blooms.

Focal Flower First

If you're having trouble deciding where to begin, start by selecting your statement flower and go from there. This might be your favorite flower or just something that jumped out at you while you were perusing the aisles. Choosing one larger bloom first and then building the rest of your arrangement around it is a great way to shop for faux florals. Go for a variety of textures, bloom shapes/sizes, and colors to complement your main flower choice. This is often the way I shop for my arrangements!

CHAPTER 2: TOOLS AND MATERIALS

Before you can start crafting with faux florals, there are some essential tools you'll need. You can make a simple arrangement using just a pair of wire cutters and a vase, but there are a variety of tools, materials, and supplies that are helpful in making beautiful, long-lasting floral arrangements and projects.

Basic Tools

Wire Cutters

You can find wire cutters made especially for working with faux florals at any craft store, but I use a heavy-duty pair of diagonal wire snips I got from a local hardware store. They are a bit more ergonomic and have more cutting power when working with thick wire and stems.

Dry Floral Foam

There are two types of floral foam: wet foam, which is used with fresh flowers, and dry foam, which is made for working with faux and dried florals. Floral foam can be cut and shaped to fit any vessel. You can use this foam as a foundation to push your stems into when creating floral arrangements.

Floral Foam Tools

Floral foam can be cut with any serrated knife you might find in your kitchen, but I found this plastic knife worked especially well. It comes in a pack with a shaping tool, which essentially acts like sandpaper to smooth and shape your foam, and a scribe tool, which is helpful for marking foam and tucking.

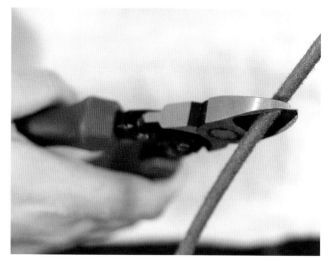

A heavy-duty pair of diagonal wire cutters is essential.

Though messy to cut and trim, dry floral foam is an important material to use for unusual vessels.

Faux floral tools: (A) floral sticky clay roll; (B) safety glasses; (C) ruler; (D) floral foam tools; (E) greening pins; (F) floral scissors; (G) floral wire; (H) floral tape; (I) safety gloves; (J) wire cutters.

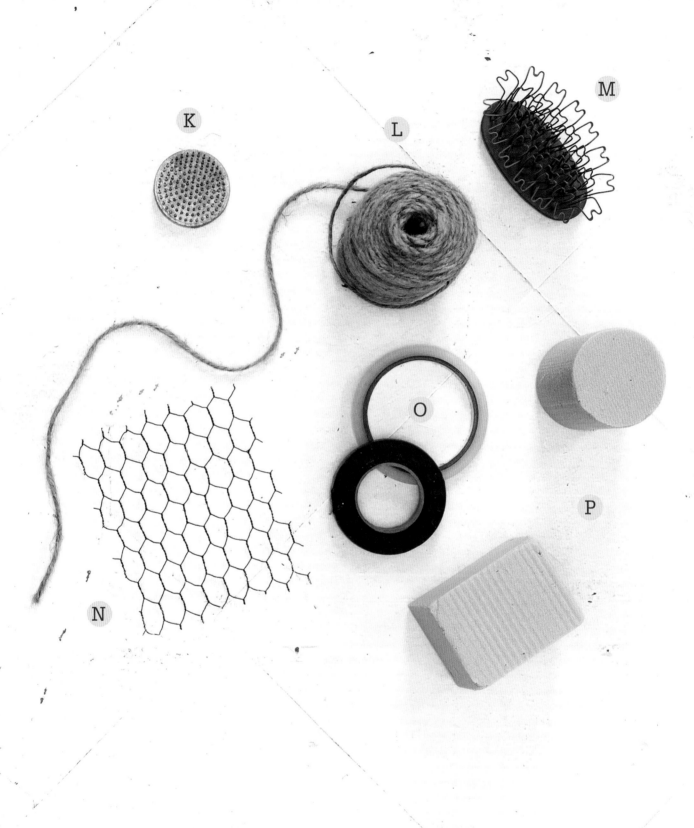

Faux floral tools: (K) traditional floral frog; (L) twine; (M) hairpin frog; (N) chicken wire; (O) floral tape; (P) dry floral foam.

Clear floral tape can be used to create a stabilizing grid on the opening of your vessel.

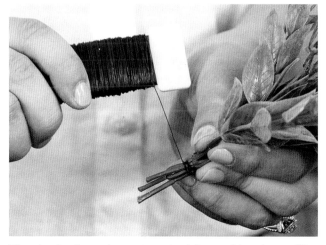

Floral wire is an important tool for making items like wreaths and garlands.

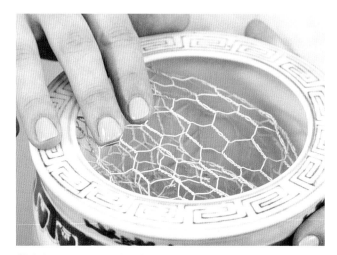

Chicken wire easily shapes to containers to keep your florals in place.

Floral Tape

There are two main types of floral tape: clear floral tape and floral stem tape. Clear floral tape can be used on its own to create a grid across the mouth of your vase for arranging flowers within. It is also useful for stabilizing your mechanics (dry floral foam, chicken wire, etc.) in your vessel. Clear floral tape is essentially the same as scotch tape, but it's packaged in a narrower roll that is versatile for floral arranging. Floral stem tape is used for holding florals together for designs that don't include a vase or for attaching shorter stems to floral wire to lengthen them. It's unlike most other types of tape because it needs to be stretched for the adhesive to activate. This ensures the floral tape sticks to itself but not your fingers. Floral stem tape comes in a variety of colors: green, brown, black, and white.

Floral Wire

Floral wire comes in sizes ranging from the thicker 16-gauge (or ¹⁄₁₆" [1.3 mm]) wire to the very thin 30-gauge (or ¹⁄₃₀" [0.25 mm]) wire. Heavier wires that range from 16 to 20 gauges can be used to support heavy flowers and replace or lengthen stems. Floral wire from 22 to 26 gauges is considered "all purpose" and is used for attaching florals to wreaths, garlands, and other types of arrangements. Very fine wire ranging from 28 to 30 gauges is mostly used for attaching ribbons, bows, or other decorative accessories.

Greening Pins

Greening pins are also known as mossing pins, U-pins, or simply floral pins. They are used for attaching foliage such as moss, leaves, bark, or other greenery to floral foam. They are made of wire that's similar to a paperclip, so they're lightweight and easy to use.

Chicken Wire

Chicken wire is a type of light wire netting that can be shaped and fit into a vessel to hold the stems of a floral arrangement in place. Specialty floral mesh is coated with rubber, so the wire will not rust when it comes into contact with water. For working with faux flowers and greenery, regular chicken wire from the hardware store will work just fine.

Floral Frog

Floral frogs are made from a variety of materials like plastic, glass, or metal and are used for holding floral arrangements in place. The two types I have pictured on page 22 are a traditional pin frog and a hairpin frog. The traditional pin frog is made of a metal base with sharp pointy wires coming up from the base. The hairpin frog is made of coated metal with looped wire (similar to a hairpin) for holding floral stems.

Hot Glue Gun

A hot glue gun comes in handy when working with faux florals. You can also use it to reattach a flower head that might pop off the stem, secure florals to a wreath form, attach a piece of moss to disguise a greening pin, and much more.

Safety Glasses

When cutting floral wire, it's a good idea to protect your eyes from any flying pieces of metal. Safety first!

Protective Gloves

It's important to wear gloves when you're handling chemicals like acrylic water. I also recommend using gloves when working with chicken wire so you can shape it without stabbing your fingers on cut ends.

Lazy Susan

Although you can certainly craft faux floral arrangements without one, I found a simple lazy Susan made it easy to turn my arrangements as I worked on them and viewed them from all angles. Any lazy Susan will do; it doesn't have to be fancy. To make the projects in this book, I used an inexpensive one I already had in my kitchen pantry.

Other Items

Depending on your project, you may want to have some other supplies on hand. Examples of these supplies are a sturdy pair of scissors for cutting tape or string, jute twine as a base if you're making a garland, rulers to quickly measure your stems before cutting if precision is necessary, etc.

This is a traditional pin frog, and they add a nice vintage design element, so don't feel like you have to cover them up.

I love these safety glasses! They have clear protective lenses on the sides that help keep my eyes protected from every angle.

Gloves are very handy when using chemicals and cutting chicken wire.

"Inspiration can strike in any little moment and be picked up from the smallest details."

—*Stephanie Kirby of The Blue Daisy Floral Designs, Pittsburgh, PA*

Wreath Forms

If a wreath is on your project list, there are several types of wreath forms to choose from: wire, grapevine, foam, straw, or simple metal hoops.

Wire

Wire wreath forms are used as a foundation for attaching bundles of florals with floral wire. Wire wreath forms are an affordable option and are lightweight and easy to hang. Because the structure of the wreath form is so simple, it may take more florals to get a full look than with some of the other options.

Grapevine

Grapevine wreaths are made from dried branches wrapped tightly into a circular shape. Floral stems can be dipped into hot glue and then pushed in between the branches to secure. Grapevine wreaths are beautiful on their own. This makes them great for asymmetrical wreaths that leave part of the vines exposed. They are inexpensive and sturdy, which makes them a popular choice for wreath making. Grapevine wreaths can be a bit limiting in terms of style and are best for more rustic, casual designs.

Foam

Foam wreath forms are a great lightweight option for creating wreaths. Florals can be attached to the wreath with greening pins and hot glue. Foam forms can also be easily covered in moss or wrapped in ribbon as a part of your design. The downside to foam forms is that they can be a bit delicate and can break if they are dropped.

Straw

Straw wreaths are not used as often as other wreath forms, but they are inexpensive and easy to work with. Florals can be attached with floral pins or hot glue and the straw helps with holding stems in place, similar to a grapevine wreath. Straw wreath forms are great for country or fall wreaths, but they aren't as versatile in style as other forms. Straw can also be a bit messy to work with.

Metal Hoop

Recently, simple metal hoops have become a popular base for modern, asymmetrical wreath designs. They come in a variety of sizes and metal finishes, most commonly silver or brass. They are perfect for a fresh, minimal look. Florals can be attached with floral wire or floral stem tape, although it can be a little tricky to secure them without sliding.

Other Options

These are the most commonly used wreath forms, but there is a wide array of non-traditional wreath forms if you want to get creative. I've seen giant wreaths made using a painted hula-hoop as a base, wreaths made with embroidery hoops, picture frames, baskets, wood slices, and bicycle wheels. The options are truly endless!

Use floral wire to attach your faux flowers and greenery to wire wreath forms.

Types of wreath forms, clockwise from top: foam, wire, straw, metal hoop, and grapevine.

CHAPTER 3: COLLECTING INSPIRATION

Look beyond faux when you're getting inspiration. My secret to creating modern, stylish faux floral arrangements is to get inspiration from what's happening in fresh floral design. You can learn so much from studying what the professionals are doing. I love to peruse the work of florists and designers on Instagram and Pinterest. If you've never crafted with faux florals before, spend some time gathering inspiration and figuring out your style first. Your finished project will be better for it. And who doesn't love looking at photos of pretty flowers? To get you started on your hunt for inspiration, I've pulled together this inspiration gallery, highlighting the work of talented makers from around the globe.

Look to online platforms like Instagram and Pinterest for inspiration.

To give your house a fresh, modern look, keep yourself updated on current trends, such as this rustic arrangement of delicate flowers and lots of greenery.

ROSEMARY & RUST

Meghan Connors and Shea Mack

Floral and Event Designers, Shrewsbury, PA

Rosemary & Rust specializes in natural, organic, and eclectic wedding and event floral design. In their quaint, small-town shop, you'll find fun, funky arrangements featuring seasonal, locally grown blooms and a selection of plants, containers, and products that fit their charming and rustic vibe.

Instagram: @RosemaryandRust   Website: *www.RosemaryandRust.com*

PHOTO CREDIT: SPARROW + LACE PHOTOGRAPHY

Rosemary & Rust's duo Shea (left) and Meghan (right) specializes in arranging florals for weddings and special events.

The combination of muted pinks, browns, and greens with off-whites in this bouquet give the arrangement a vintage look.

These boutonnieres are simple but elegant.

The eucalyptus leaves and white roses in these bouquets match the bride's a bridal party's dress colors, and the addition of light pink ranunculus gives it subtle pop of color.

The tight buds of the flowers set against the leafy, wild greenery come together to create this romantic bouquet.

Favorite flowers:
We love all flowers, but a few of our favorites are peonies, scabiosa, blue delphinium, and garden roses.

Best advice on floral design:
The best advice is to just play with flowers! They make their own beauty in so many ways that you are only adding to that as you arrange them, whether strategically or whimsically.

On working with faux:
Spend a little bit of extra money to get the florals that will have longevity. Some of the cheaper options will fade faster, fray at the edges, and not hold up over time. Investing in quality faux florals and keeping them cobweb- and dust-free will keep your arrangement looking as good as the day you made it.

BROOKLYN BLOOMS

LaParis Phillips

Professional Florist, Brooklyn, NY

Brooklyn Blooms is known for infusing their love of fashion, art, and culture into their designs by combining unexpected textures, colors, and flowers together.

Instagram: @BrooklynBloomsNYC   Website: *www.BrooklynBlooms.com*

Brooklyn Blooms's LaParis Phillips styles her arrangements in fun, unexpected ways, even down to the vessel in which she displays them.

This arrangement—called "The Chauncey"—was created with bold textures and unconventional flowers.

PHOTO CREDIT: JASON SPEAR

- **Favorite flowers:**

  I always say that I don't have one—like seriously, how do I choose? However, if I HAD to choose, I would have to say the underrated and underestimated carnation. Carnations are making a comeback in a major way with various beautiful novelty colors being created. They are also cost-effective and extremely long lasting!

- **What makes her style unique:**

  I love creating unexpected color palettes and changing the perspective on what "matches." I love painting designs on leaves to add another unexpected pop of color and texture.

- **Best advice on floral design:**

  It's okay to start over if you're not happy with your arrangement. Sometimes you have to destroy and rebuild to get a better result. I've been designing for fourteen years, and I'm still learning. Never stop being a student, not only in floristry, but in life as well!

Adding designs on boutonnieres like this is a way Brooklyn Blooms uses simple artistic touches to personalize items for their customers.

The array of colors in this arrangement pairs perfectly with the vintage bronze vase it sits in.

The designs Brooklyn Blooms adds to their arrangements give their floral arrangements a fun, modern twist.

Combining colorful carnations—Phillips's current favorite flower—with colorful leaf designs and a classic white vase creates a chic, contemporary arrangement.

THE MACADAMIA SHOP

Eveline Leake

Faux Floral Designer, Clifton Park, NY

The Macadamia Shop is known for one-of-a-kind faux floral arrangements, wreaths, and a curated selection of home goods available through their website.

Instagram: @TheMacadamiaShop   Website: *www.TheMacadamiaShop.com*

PHOTO CREDIT: EVELINE LEAKE

The Macadamia Shop's Eveline Leake creates faux flowers, plants, and signs to help her customers make their house a "home sweet home."

Though this arrangement looks super colorful, it uses a simple array of pinks, oranges, and whites.

- **Favorite flowers:**
  Peonies, although I've been in love with dahlias lately.

- **Best advice on floral design:**
  Know where to stop. It seems so basic, yet lots of people have problems with that. Arranging flowers (faux or fresh) is an art. Your arrangement needs to have a focal point but also be balanced with a variety of different textures and colors and also a little blank space. Instead of being overwhelming, it's about being beautifully balanced.

- **On working with faux:**
  I'm a floral everything kind of girl, always loved having flowers at home. But it isn't easy to find the flowers I love all year long where I live in upstate NY. Having realistic-looking faux flowers brings me the same happy feeling every time I look at them!

This round black vase works well to show off the linear pastel floral arrangement it holds.

Faux flower arrangements can include surprising elements, such as the pears and berries used in this wreath.

Creating arrangements with faux florals allows you the freedom to use unique, pretty vases like this mint blue one here.

GOOSEBERRY HILL FARM

Anna Falkon

Farmer and Florist, Adelaide Hills, South Australia

Gooseberry Hill Farm is known for organically grown, seasonal cut flowers, and artfully designed wedding florals. In addition to flowers, Anna and her family also raise sheep, and she makes beautiful, naturally dyed silk ribbons (and sometimes clothes) in small batches with leftover flower and plant material.

Instagram: @GooseberryHillFlowers   Website: *www.GooseberryHillFarm.com.au*

PHOTO CREDIT: ELIZABETH DENNING

Anna Falkon loves to create Gooseberry Hill Farm's beautiful organic arrangements by working with any floral imperfections in a creative way.

The muted colors of this arrangement allows the flowing design and large blooms to take center stage.

This collection of arrangements varies in size and height but the pieces are all still tied together with their similarities in color.

Colors like the burnt orange and autumn peach flowers in this arrangement are some of Falkon's favorites.

- **Favorite flowers:**
  That's like asking my favorite child! It definitely changes with the seasons, and also year by year. As I am writing this, heirloom chrysanthemum season has just started in South Australia, so I'm loving them, in all their muted autumn shades. High up on the list all year and every year are bearded iris, and, of course, fragrant garden roses, always!

- **Best advice on floral design:**
  I met Katie Davis of Ponderosa & Thyme at one of her workshops last year, and as we were choosing our flowers, she said, "Remember, guys, green is a color." I've always struggled with green in my work and found that sometimes I carefully curate a palette, and then if I added greenery it completely changes everything. Green is good for some arrangements, and not so good for others. Rather than "bulking out" arrangements with plain greenery, I often use colored foliage or dried elements to add texture, and I try to work with negative space instead.

- **Current color scheme crush:**
  I love all colors! A constant (and definitely a comfort zone) is probably the autumn-y peach, burnt orange, rust, and bronzy range. Lately, I've also been loving yellow—on its own or with pink or purple.

This unique trailing arrangement displays Falkon's unapologetically wild style.

THE BLUE DAISY FLORAL DESIGNS

Stephanie Kirby

Professional Florist, Pittsburgh, PA

The Blue Daisy Floral Designs is known for its romantic, English Garden floral design style that beautifully blends color, texture, and fragrance, while finding the balance between current trends and transcending time.

Instagram: @TheBlueDaisyFloral   Website: *www.TheBlueDaisyFloral.com*

PHOTO CREDIT: APRIL HUBAL

Stephanie Kirby, owner and creative director at The Blue Daisy Floral Designs, has loved flowers since she was a young child helping her mother in the garden.

This romantic arrangement
mainly contains pastel flowers
but also uses pops of deep reds
and purples throughout.

- **Favorite flower:**
  Tulips. They come in so many colors, varieties, and textures. And they're rebels! They are always changing shape and position over time in an arrangement as they grow and stretch toward the light.

- **Best advice on floral design:**
  Work *with* the flowers, not *against* them. If a stem has a particular curve or a branch a unique shape, figure out how to use it to make the design more interesting! Also, the old adage "measure twice and cut once" definitely applies to working with fresh or permanent botanicals.

- **Trick of the trade:**
  Design your arrangement so the florals are two-thirds and the vessel is one-third of the entire design. This is a good basic principle to follow when getting started. Though, I also believe that once you've mastered the rules, you can break them!

An abundance of light, big-bloomed flowers combined with small greenery pieces placed here and there gives this arrangement its dreamy look.

This bridal bouquet is pretty in pink, yellow, and cream.

The overflowing design, skinny vase, and mixture of light and dark blooms all come together to create this dramatic arrangement.

THE ROGUE PETAL CO.

Alyssa Grogan

Faux Floral Designer, Baltimore, MD

The Rogue Petal Co. designs faux florals for any occasion, and is best known for its realistic wedding arrangements that are reasonably priced; like bouquets, boutonnieres, and flower crowns. At Rouge Petal Co., they also love to make home arrangements and floral pieces for human and fur babies!

Instagram: @RoguePetalCo   Website: *www.RoguePetalCo.com*

PHOTO CREDIT: ALYSSA GROGAN

The Rogue Petal Co.'s Alyssa Grogan became inspired to start her faux floral company after she had her own cost-effective wedding using silk flowers.

The dark and light flower colors create the romantic, untraditional look for this bouquet.

The use of large dark purple blooms and lighter, smaller flowers allows the light blooms to really pop.

The red and orange berries provide a unique foundation for the flowers, while the wild leafy greenery contrasts wonderfully with the tightly bundled floral arrangement.

By placing the dark pink focal flower off to the side and trailing the lighter flowers in a "C" shape next to it, this arrangement feels very balanced.

- **Favorite flowers:**
  All types of thistle. I try to squeeze it into as many designs as possible! I also adore cabbage roses.

- **Best advice on floral design:**
  Floral design is an art form: the flowers are your tools and you are the artist. The more you practice putting arrangements together, you will find a style or two that you prefer. As a florist, it's okay to say no to a design that doesn't represent your style or vision. Whether you are arranging flowers for a business, for you, or just for the sake of creating (those are the best), you will be most proud of the end product if you followed your favorite style or method.

- **On working with faux:**
  I designed faux arrangements for my own wedding and quickly became obsessed with the arranging and creating. I have always been an artist and crafter, but I discovered my passion after the flowers turned out so lovely and no one could tell they were fake!

The various pinks and off-whites in this centerpiece work beautifully with the golds and pinks of this table arrangement for pretty, feminine décor.

LORRAINE'S COTTAGE

Stephanie Petrak

Faux Floral Designer, Cleveland, OH

Lorraine's Cottage is an online boutique established in 2014 and is loved for its handmade, lush, and whimsical faux floral wreaths, garlands, and arrangements.

Instagram: @LorCottage   Website: *www.LorrainesCottage.com*

PHOTO CREDIT: STEPHANIE PETRAK

Lorraine's Cottage owner, Stephanie Petrak, creates faux floral arrangements for the home so her customers can enjoy beautiful flowers year round.

By balancing the pink and white roses on either side of the dark hydrangea focal flower, this wreath feels symmetrical without seeming too perfect.

PHOTO CREDIT: STEPHANIE PETRAK

- **Favorite flowers:**
  Blue and green hydrangeas. When I was a child, they grew in my backyard, and I've loved the big, fluffy blooms ever since.

- **Best advice on floral design:**
  Make sure your arrangement doesn't look like a clump by giving it some movement. An arrangement can have more interest and a modern touch if you go beyond the traditional globe shape. Most importantly, always go with your creative spirit because floral arranging is an art form.

- **On her design formula:**
  I always have a focal flower that's not right in the center of the arrangement, and I always make sure to have some whimsical, free-flowing element in the arrangement, like trailing greenery or a long bouncy floral stem.

The beauty of this arrangement comes from placing the delicate greens and large blooms in a metallic gold and white vase.

To achieve an asymmetrical look in this arrangement, the blush pink roses and light blue hydrangeas were placed in a triangular shape off to the side.

The use of a mixture of greenery in this wreath lends it a wild look.

This beautiful arrangement looks rustic and untamed due to the wild greenery and pink florals.

"In the past, faux flowers consisted mainly of blatantly fake, boisterous colored stems. However, now you can find pieces that look so real you have to touch them a few times to double-check that they are faux. There have been a handful of times I've accidentally leaned into a bin of craft stems to smell them because I forgot they were artificial for a second!"

—*Alyssa Grogan of The Rogue Petal Co., Baltimore, MD*

PART II:
DECORATING WITH FAUX FLOWERS

Decorating with faux flowers is particularly great for those who don't have a "green thumb," or those who don't have the time for real plants.

CHAPTER 4: FRESH AND FAUX

Fresh or faux? When decorating your home with botanicals, use both fresh and faux florals and greenery. There are some places where fresh cut flowers and live plants work well and other instances where faux is simply a better fit. I do enjoy tending to houseplants, but I found I have the best results happen if I limit the number to just a few. So, I mostly keep my live plants in my sunniest room (my studio) and decorate the rest of my home with realistic faux plants.

Decorating with plants is a great way to bring life to a room, but sometimes an empty corner that needs a little something visually doesn't have the appropriate amount of light for a houseplant. Create your own faux plants to decorate shelves and dark corners that are not ideal for live plants. Using faux in these instances is the best of both worlds—you get the beauty and movement of a live plant without having to worry about inadequate growing conditions.

Placing a seasonal centerpiece on your dinner table, like this autumnal arrangement (see page 132), will help bring warmth and cheer into your home.

Decorate your home with both fresh and faux florals; just be sure to keep the lighting conditions in mind when doing so.

Going faux for floral arrangements is a great idea if you love entertaining. Most party preparation, like making food, must be done within a day or so of the event. But if you use faux flowers for your centerpieces and décor, you can get ahead on your to-do list and craft those well ahead of time. Faux flowers are perfect for the holidays if you're hosting multiple get-togethers. You can make one arrangement that can last all season long.

In addition to party décor, you can use a faux floral arrangement anywhere you would use a fresh one: as a centerpiece on your dining table or an accent in your living room, in a bud vase on your bathroom counter, a small arrangement on your bedroom nightstand, etc. Statement arrangements and centerpieces can be changed seasonally, but simple groupings of all one type and color of bloom can look beautiful in an interior setting all year round. I'm partial to white flowers because I tend to decorate with neutrals, but choose whatever colors you love that fit with the style of your décor. If your style is bright and airy, a vase of pale pink peonies would be a lovely permanent addition to a console table. If you're style is bolder and more bohemian, a tall vase of red gladiolus would be a striking focal point in a living room. Or if you're like me and favor neutrals, go for a simple vase brimming with white hydrangeas or Queen Anne's lace.

For a classic, timeless style, I always look to nature for inspiration. Flowers come in every hue, but when decorating my home with faux I'm most drawn to shades and varieties that look like they could have been plucked from an English cottage–style garden. Even just a few leafy branches in a jug can add a lot of interest to a corner. A simple and natural look is always timeless.

Using faux flowers for your party décor can help you get ahead of your schedule and save time to complete more important tasks.

"In my experience, the most successful designs for home florals are less complex than those for wedding bouquets. You can create a floral accent piece made up of only greenery or a single branch or flower you adore to pretty up your space. You are using the arrangement(s) to accent a room, not be the focus necessarily."

—*Alyssa Grogan of The Rogue Petal Co., Baltimore, MD*

Cleaning and Maintenance

The best thing you can do for the maintenance of your faux flower projects is to invest in quality materials from the beginning. The better quality you use, the more longevity you will get out of your arrangement. Some of the cheaper options are more prone to fading or fraying at the edges and in general won't hold up as well over time.

To maintain your faux flowers, dust them periodically and clean them with an artificial flower cleaner/treatment. Using canned air is a great way to quickly dust an arrangement. To extend the life of a wreath or project that will be outdoors, you can purchase UV protectant spray that's made for artificial flowers and greenery. If you have a covered porch, that may not be necessary. As always, use your judgment.

"Take care of your silk flowers. They will last a very long time and be well worth the investment. You can reinvent them as styles change by adding to or reworking the shape or fully pull apart your creation after a few years and maybe transform it into a wreath for your sun porch!"

—*Meghan Connors and Shea Mack of Rosemary & Rust, Shrewsbury, PA*

Investing in quality faux florals and keeping them free of cobwebs and dust will keep your arrangement looking as good as the day you made it.

CHAPTER 5: FLORAL DESIGN FUNDAMENTALS

Principles of Design

One thing I remember learning in my Art Fundamentals class during my freshman year of design school is that "design is design." Whether it's fine art, interior design, product design, or floral design, all good design comes from the same basic principles: proportion, scale, rhythm, balance, unity, and emphasis.

Balance

This principle refers to the way in which the visual weight of an arrangement is distributed. Balance can be achieved by one of three methods: *symmetry*, *asymmetry*, and *radial symmetry*. In a symmetrical arrangement, both sides of the composition will mirror each other from left to right. In an asymmetrical arrangement, the two sides will be different from each other but balanced through repetition or contrast (e.g., one large element being balanced on the other side with a grouping of small). Radial symmetry is achieved my mirroring a composition on more than one axis. So instead of looking left to right, imagine looking at an arrangement from the top down and seeing a vertical and horizontal axis intersecting at a fixed center point. Floral elements are spaced equally around the center point like the spokes of a wheel. Radial symmetry is a classic composition for floral arrangements and often gives a more formal and elegant feel.

This arrangement is a good example of radial symmetry.

When creating floral arrangements, follow
the basic design principles of proportion,
scale, rhythm, balance, unity, and emphasis.

The contrast of the white magnolias against a background of green foliage makes the flowers the focal point in this garland.

Emphasis

Emphasis means creating a focal point or points in a composition. This is often done through contrasting the size, color, texture, or shape of an element from the other elements surrounding it. For example, a focal point can be created by placing one large bloom near the front of the arrangement and surrounding it with smaller flowers and berries that contrast in size and texture. Another way to create a focal point is to use a bold color against a background of mostly greenery and light-colored flowers. The shape of an arrangement can also be used to create a focal point. Perhaps you place three large blooms in a triangle as the focal point for an asymmetrical arrangement.

Rhythm

Rhythm is created by repeating elements in a composition in a way that implies movement or pattern. Repeating the same floral element across an arrangement in a triangular or diagonal shape is a good way to achieve rhythm and movement. Rhythm can be established in both symmetrical and asymmetrical arrangements by repeating the same flower in several locations across the composition.

The marigolds in this arrangement are placed in a triangular shape to achieve rhythm.

Make sure your arrangement is taller than your vase.

Proportion

This principle refers to the way the separate elements of a composition relate to each other in size. Although it's good to play with contrasting sizes for variety, the vessel, flowers, and foliage need to be close enough in scale to create harmony. As a general rule, the highest point of your arrangement should be one to two times the height of your vase.

Scale

Scale is like proportion but refers to the size of the arrangement in relation to its setting. As an interior designer, this part is very important to me. If you're making a centerpiece, make sure your vessel and arrangement is large enough to really make a statement on your table. If you're making a wreath, choose a wreath form wide enough for the scale of your door. (A good rule of thumb is to have a finished width of 18"–20" [45.7–50.8cm].)

Unity

Unity is achieved when the other design principles are considered and executed well. The goal is for the composition as a whole is to be greater than the sum of its parts. Flowers, foliage, and vessel should blend together harmoniously and be suited to the setting in a visually pleasing way.

Always make sure you create proportional arrangements and wreaths to fit where you plan on placing them.

Although there are several different colors in this arrangement, they all blend together to make a visually pleasing holiday table centerpiece.

"I approach each arrangement as a piece
of art; flowers add character to any space
they're in. I want it to be interesting to
look at from every angle. Dimension and
movement are key to me."

—*LaParis Phillips of Brooklyn Blooms, Brooklyn, NY*

My Basic Formula: Frame, Foundation, Focal, and Filler

In studying floral design for this book, I found that many florists use a type of formula when creating their arrangements. There are many versions with varying terminology out there, but the essence of this formula is always the same.

Frame

The frame is the hidden structure of the arrangement. In floral design, this is referred to as your mechanics. Depending on the vessel and the type of arrangement you are creating, there are many different techniques and methods to choose from. Starting on page 76, I've shared how to use a floral tape grid, chicken wire form, floral foam, and a floral pin frog step-by-step.

You may find it useful to draw your arrangement first to determine that you've followed the formula correctly.

"Your arrangement needs to have a focal point but also be balanced with a variety of different textures and colors and also a little blank space."

—*Eveline Leake of The Macadamia Shop, Clifton Park, NY*

Foundation

The foundation of an arrangement is your greenery and foliage. Placing leaves and branches at the base of your arrangement does two things: It helps to cover the mouth of your vessel and hide your mechanics, and it adds a natural feel to your arrangement since flowers are usually surrounded by leaves in nature. Choose greenery that is complementary in color and shape to the flowers and other botanical elements in your arrangement.

Your choice of greenery helps to shape the overall arrangement both in style and shape. Where you place your first few stems of greenery will help determine the height and balance of your arrangement. There are a couple questions you want to consider while you are placing your greenery: Do you want your arrangement to be low and wide or tall and fountain-like? Round and symmetrical or more irregularly shaped and asymmetrical? Where you place your greenery creates the foundation for the rest of your arrangement and will inform where you'll place your focal point.

From left to right: ficus, euonymus, fern, baby blue eucalyptus, lamb's ear, juniper, seeded eucalyptus, and olive.

Focal

Your focal flowers are usually your largest flowers, with blooms measuring at least 3"–6" (7.6–15.25 cm) in diameter. These flowers are meant to catch your attention and create a focal point (or points) in your arrangement. The placement of your focal flowers will guide the rest of the arrangement. Think about putting your focal point slightly off-center or using multiple focal points to create movement in your design. To mimic the way flowers grow in nature, place your focal flowers in groupings of two or three. As a general rule, using odd numbers of focal flowers (like three, five, seven, etc.) are the most pleasing to the eye.

TIP
The tallest point of your arrangement should be somewhere between one and two times the height of your vessel.

From left to right: white, pink, and purple roses; yellow ranunculus; cream hydrangea; red poppy; pink peony; white magnolia; mauve dahlia; and red geranium.

Filler

Filler flowers do just that—fill in the empty spots and add fullness to your overall arrangement. Filler flowers can be branched stems or sprays with multiple blooms that measure about ¼"–½" (0.65–1.3 cm) in diameter, or they can be groupings of medium-sized flowers that are about 1½"–3" (3.8–7.6 cm) in diameter. Medium-sized blooms act as supporting flowers to the focal flower, whereas smaller sprays and berries act as a more textural element.

A lot of this classification also has to do with the overall size of your arrangement. Some medium-sized flowers can be focal flowers in a smaller arrangement and filler flowers in a larger arrangement. Just make sure to choose filler flowers that are smaller than the focal flower, but other than that, there is a lot of room to be creative with your filler choices.

Think about using more unexpected elements such as fruit, branches, grasses, and even fabric butterflies or insects in your project. In my fall centerpiece on page 132, I used both plums and skimmia berries as filler. In a spring or summer arrangement, you could use lemon or orange branches. In a fall or winter arrangement, you could use apples, artichokes, or cabbage for a unique addition to your project.

TIP
Bend and shape stems for a more natural look, allowing some leaves and flowers to dip below the line of the vase so it looks like they are spilling out. This makes your arrangement look less stiff and more organic.

The small blue lupine sprays, small white buttercups, and the medium yellow and orange poppies are the filler flowers in this arrangement.

"Mixing textures, colors, and silhouettes applies to arranging flowers just as much as it applies to creating the perfect look."

—*LaParis Phillips of Brooklyn Blooms, Brooklyn, NY*

Choosing a Vessel

Almost anything can be a vessel, especially for faux florals, which don't need water. Think beyond the vase! I like to shop at thrift stores to find unique vessels for my craft projects. In my fall centerpiece project, I arranged my florals in an old trophy; in my winter centerpiece, I used a vintage soup tureen.

It's also fun to reimagine items you already have. For my summer succulent garden project (see page 124), I used a decorative birdcage I've had for almost a decade that was previously gathering dust in a closet. With a fresh coat of paint, I repurposed it into a hanging planter.

If you are using a glass vase, keep your arrangement modern and understated by skipping common vase fillers such as marbles, pebbles, or faux gems. Instead, use acrylic water (see technique on page 84) to get a more natural look or forgo filler altogether. This is a personal preference, but I think simplicity is best.

TIP
Keep in mind the diameter of the mouth of your vessel. This determines how many flowers you'll need. The wider the mouth, the more flowers you will need to keep your arrangement looking full.

Cut your stems at an angle for a more realistic look. This is especially important if you're using a clear vase. An angled cut also makes it easier to push stems into floral foam.

Color Schemes to Try

The best color scheme to use for your craft project is the one that speaks to you! But if you're feeling stuck, here's some inspiration for tried-and-true color combinations: monochromatic, complementary, analogous, and triadic.

Monochromatic

Monochromatic arrangements feature flowers that are all the same color. For a pleasing variety, use different shades of the same color. For example, if you want to use all pink flowers in your arrangement, try mixing pastel blush tones with deeper roses and mauves. When I'm working with one color family, I usually like to add a bit of contrast with a few white or neutral flowers and some greenery. For a true monochromatic arrangement, you can get creative with your foliage. Pink flowers with red maple leaves would be stunning.

Analogous

Analogous color schemes feature three or more colors that are situated next to each other on the color wheel, including primary, secondary, and tertiary colors. For example, you can feature red-orange, orange, and yellow-orange flowers together for a warm-toned arrangement or blue, blue violet, and violet for a cool-toned arrangement. Choose three colors in a row from anywhere on the color wheel for a scheme that will blend together nicely.

Complementary

For a bold and striking arrangement, try pairing colors that sit opposite to each other on the color wheel. Through this contrast, each flower's hue will appear even more vibrant. The three primary-secondary complements are violet and yellow, blue and orange, and red and green. For something a little different, try pairing tertiary complements such as blue green and red orange, yellow green and red violet, and blue violet and yellow orange.

Triadic

If you love bold color, a triadic color scheme might be the one for you. These schemes feature three colors that are spaced equidistantly on the color wheel, forming a triangle. It sounds complicated, but it's actually easy to figure out once you know this trick.

When you're looking at a color wheel, you can draw an imaginary triangle between red, yellow, and blue. This is the primary triad. Another imaginary triangle can be drawn between violet, orange, and green. This is the secondary triad. To find a tertiary triad, just take either the primary or secondary triad and move each of the points of the imaginary triangle one space to the left or right on the color wheel. I personally love the combination of yellow green, red orange, and blue violet in floral arrangements.

When choosing the color scheme for your arrangement, consider one of the following combinations: monochromatic, complementary, analogous, and triadic.

Floral Arranging Techniques

Depending on the type of vessel you choose, you may or may not need to use an additional structural element as the foundation for your floral arrangement. On pages 20–26, I described the different types of floral arrangement mechanics. In this section, I'll show you how to use them, step by step.

Floral Tape Grid

Using floral tape to create your own grid is the most affordable and flexible way to structure a tabletop arrangement. Floral tape can be bought in clear or green colors. Clear is for using with glass vessels and green can be used to grid the top of opaque vessels. It also has many other uses, such as elongating shorter stems by attaching them to floral wire. Floral tape is usually about ¼" (0.65cm) wide, which is an ideal thickness for a wide variety of vessel sizes, but in a pinch even Scotch tape will do just fine.

SUPPLIES
- Clear floral tape
- Vessel of your choice
- Scissors
- Faux florals or greenery

1. Find the center point of your vase and lay two lines of tape on either side of it—about ½"–1" (1.3–2.55cm) apart, depending on the size of your vase.

2. Continue laying parallel tape lines across the width of your vase.

3. Turn your vase 90 degrees and repeat steps 1 and 2 to create a grid.

4. Run a piece of clear tape around the outer rim of your vase to secure the tape ends.

5. Place your florals inside the grid as desired.

TIP

In addition to making your own grid from tape, you can also purchase premade wire flower arrangers that do the same thing.

Chicken Wire

At craft stores, you can find floral mesh that's coated in plastic to prevent rust when in contact with water. For faux arrangements, chicken wire from the hardware store works just as well. When folded to shape, the grid of the chicken wire will create a web that will securely hold your florals in place. The great thing about chicken wire is that it can be unfolded and reused for another arrangement later on, whereas materials such as tape and foam are for one use only.

SUPPLIES
- Chicken wire
- Protective gloves
- Wire cutters
- Clear floral tape
- Vessel of your choice
- Faux florals or greenery

1. Cut the chicken wire to about two times the width of your vessel. Roll the ends in toward each other.

2. Tuck in the ends, working with the chicken wire until it forms a ball shape.

3. Push your chicken wire ball into your vessel and continue forming it to shape. For extra security, make sure that both the top and bottom layers of your ball have open chicken wire for the floral stems to pass through the two layers.

4. Run a piece of clear tape across the mouth of the vessel to secure.

5. Place your florals inside the chicken wire as desired.

For faux florals, any kind of floral mesh or chicken wire can be used since there is no risk of rust.

Floral Foam

Floral foam can be purchased anywhere craft supplies are sold and comes in both wet (for fresh floral arrangements) and dry (for faux floral arrangements). Foam can be easily cut to fit your vessel with a serrated knife. The foam creates a sturdy structure for inserting stems at various angles. However, you want to be careful in thinking through the placement of your flowers before you push them into the foam. Removing and then relocating stems can start to degrade the structure of the foam. If you move around your florals too much, you may need to start over with a fresh piece of foam.

SUPPLIES

- Dry floral foam
- Serrated foam knife
- Foam shaping tool
- Vessel of your choice
- Rubber mallet
- Hot glue gun or heavy-duty glue
- Moss
- Greening pins
- Faux florals or greenery

1. Measure and cut the foam to fit your vessel.

2. Push or tap the foam into the vessel using a rubber mallet. If the fit isn't tight enough to secure your foam, use hot glue or a heavy-duty glue (such as E6000®) to secure it to your vessel. You may have to use multiple pieces of foam for a snug fit.

3. Cover the foam with moss using greening pins. *Optional:* To disguise greening pins, use a dab of hot glue and small clump of moss on top.

4. Insert your plant and adjust the leaves and stems to your liking.

TIP
Dry floral foam is
MESSY. I found that
using a dusting cloth
made for a dry mop was
a great way to remove
fine foam dust from
my worktop and
my vessel.

Floral Pin Frog

Before floral foam was invented, floral frogs were commonly used to hold arrangements in place. There is a wide variety of floral frogs available, made from materials like plastic, glass, or metal. My favorite type of frog to use is a metal pin frog. There are two varieties: a hairpin frog where the floral stems pass through a series of wire loops to hold them in place; and a classic pin frog, which has short, spiky pins that stems are pushed through or between. Classic pin frogs are relatively affordable and easy to find. You can use a pin frog in almost any wide-mouth vessel. I like to use them in clear glass vessels, such as compotes, so that the frog is visible in the finished arrangement.

SUPPLIES
- Pin frog
- Floral clay
- Vessel of your choice
- Faux florals or greenery

2. Place the frog in the vessel.

3. Push down and twist to secure.

1. Press the floral clay onto the backside of your pin frog where it will meet the vessel.

4. Place your florals into the frog as desired, pushing stems in between or onto pins to secure (depending on stem diameter).

Pin frogs are pretty enough to keep them displayed in a clear glass vessel as a part of your finished arrangement.

Acrylic Water

For an extra realistic touch, acrylic water is a great addition to any arrangement in a clear glass vessel. Acrylic water kits can be purchased at most craft stores and are very simple to use. Acrylic does make your arrangement permanent, so I wouldn't suggest using it in a vessel you'd like to reuse. I prefer acrylic water over other types of vase filler because it gives a more natural, streamlined, and modern look.

SUPPLIES

- Acrylic water kit
- Protective gloves
- Disposable plastic cup
- Disposable stirring stick
- Vessel of your choice
- Faux florals or greenery

1. Pour both bottles of the acrylic water kit into a disposable cup.

2. Stir for 3 minutes, following the manufacturer's recommendations.

3. Pour the solution into the vessel.

4. Place the stems as desired and put your arrangement in a safe place where it will not be disturbed for at least 12 hours while it cures.

TIP

Use clear floral tape across the mouth of your vessel to secure your florals until the acrylic fully cures, which takes about 24 hours.

Acrylic water is my favorite type of vase filler because it looks the most realistic.

Basic Wreath

In the next part of this book, I'll be sharing inspiration for four different seasonal wreaths using a variety of techniques. But first, I want to show you the basics of making your own wreath using a wire wreath form. This project may seem intimidating, but it's simple! I chose to use foliage and small berries for my wreath, but this same technique could be used for a mix of greenery and larger flowers or a full floral wreath.

SUPPLIES

- Faux florals or greenery
- Wire wreath form
- Floral wire or floral tape
- Wire cutters (if using floral wire)
- Hot glue gun

1. Cut your faux floral bushes down to individual stems and sprays, about 6"–8" (15.25–20.30cm) in length. Bundle the stems and sprays together and secure by wrapping a thin gauge floral wire tightly around the base. Floral tape also works well to fasten bundles together.

2. Attach floral wire to the wreath form by wrapping it around and through the rings several times.

3. Place your first bundle and pass the wire around it tightly several times to secure.

4. Place your next bundle, slightly overlapping the first to hide the stems, and secure. Repeat this until your entire wreath is covered. Fill in any sparse spots with extra greenery and a dab of hot glue.

Wreaths are so versatile and customizable that you can easily make one for every season.

Basic Garland

Garlands are a great addition to any décor, for parties or as an everyday part of your scheme. Making a garland is simpler than it looks, and you can customize it to any season. Make it from all greenery, all flowers, or a mixture of both. The options are endless!

SUPPLIES
- Twine
- Floral wire or floral tape
- Faux florals or greenery

1. Cut your floral bushes down to individual stems and sprays, about 6"–8" (15.25–20.30cm) in length. Bundle together and secure by wrapping a thin-gauge floral wire tightly around the base. A floral tape also works well to fasten bundles together.

2. Place your first bundle onto your length of twine and pass the wire around it tightly several times to secure.

3. Place your next bundle, slightly overlapping the first to hide the stems, and secure. Repeat this until your second to last bundle.

4. Place your last bundle in the opposite direction to the rest of your garland to hide the stems and create a finished end. It might take some adjustments to get the last few bundles to flow together. Fill in any sparse spots with extra greenery and a dab of hot glue.

Don't limit yourself to only making garland for the holidays! Garland can be used year round as a part of your normal décor scheme or to add that little extra touch to parties.

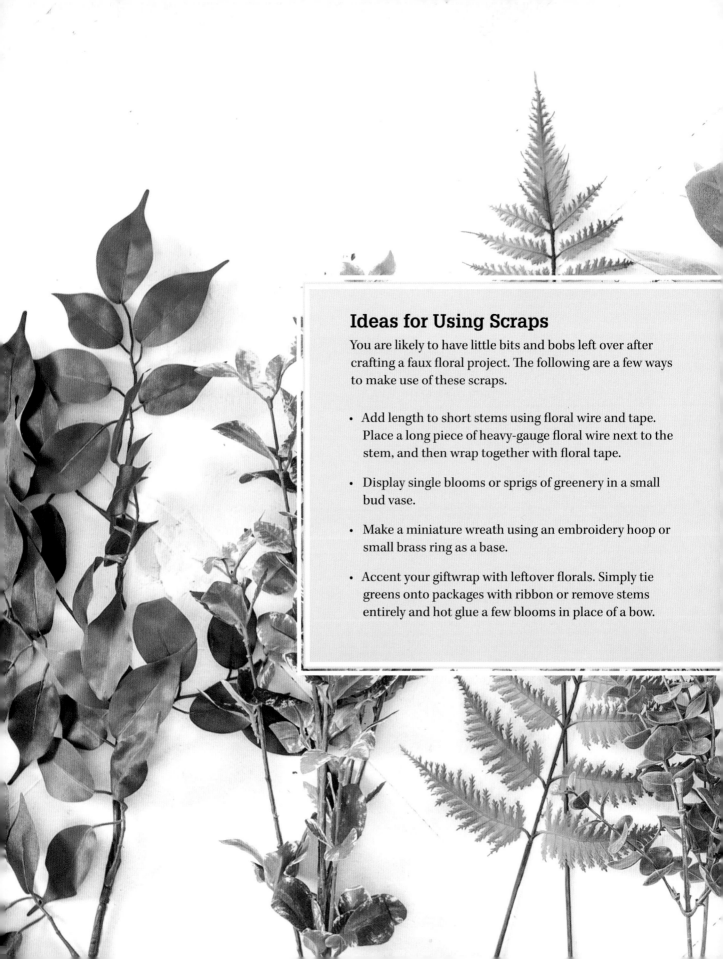

Ideas for Using Scraps

You are likely to have little bits and bobs left over after crafting a faux floral project. The following are a few ways to make use of these scraps.

- Add length to short stems using floral wire and tape. Place a long piece of heavy-gauge floral wire next to the stem, and then wrap together with floral tape.

- Display single blooms or sprigs of greenery in a small bud vase.

- Make a miniature wreath using an embroidery hoop or small brass ring as a base.

- Accent your giftwrap with leftover florals. Simply tie greens onto packages with ribbon or remove stems entirely and hot glue a few blooms in place of a bow.

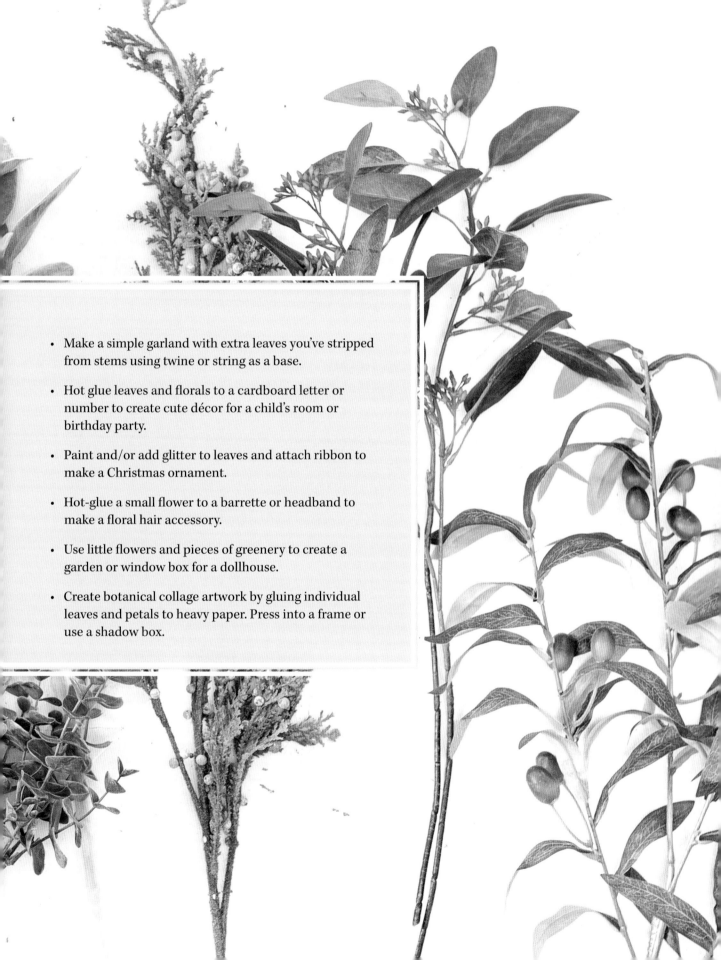

- Make a simple garland with extra leaves you've stripped from stems using twine or string as a base.

- Hot glue leaves and florals to a cardboard letter or number to create cute décor for a child's room or birthday party.

- Paint and/or add glitter to leaves and attach ribbon to make a Christmas ornament.

- Hot-glue a small flower to a barrette or headband to make a floral hair accessory.

- Use little flowers and pieces of greenery to create a garden or window box for a dollhouse.

- Create botanical collage artwork by gluing individual leaves and petals to heavy paper. Press into a frame or use a shadow box.

PART III:
PROJECTS

See page 132 to make the Autumnal Fruit and Foliage centerpiece, which is now one of my favorite arrangements.

As I've mentioned before, nature is a big inspiration to me when crafting with faux flowers. So, I thought what better way to organize the projects in this book than by season!

In the first half of the book, I shared the general tips and techniques I've learned along the way for working with faux florals and greenery. In this next section, you'll find crafting inspiration for floral arrangements, wreaths, and unique home décor projects for spring, summer, fall, and winter. I hope these projects inspire you to try your hand at crafting with faux flowers! I've included instructions for how to recreate each project, but I encourage you to be creative and customize these designs according to your own personal style, favorite flowers, and color schemes.

CHAPTER 6:
SPRING

Since spring is the season of new growth, you can really have a lot of fun with crafting faux flower and greenery projects for this season. See page 106 to see how I made this faux herb garden.

Classic Lilacs and Tulips

I'm sure I'm not the only one who looks forward to lilac season every year! In my own garden, I have a purple lilac bush that was propagated over generations by my grandmother and then me from the original lilac bush at my great-grandparents' farm in Baltimore, MD. So, needless to say, lilacs are pretty special to me.

Their tall, columnar blossoms create such a beautiful shape, both in the garden and in a vase. Real lilacs, however, bloom for a short window of time during late spring here in Pennsylvania, and my cut lilacs only seem to last about three to four days before they wilt away.

To complement the lilacs, I added other springtime favorites—tulips and waxflower. With this project, I wanted to extend the joy of springtime and lilac season all year round. It makes a great, casual centerpiece for a dining table or would look lovely sitting on your kitchen counter.

SUPPLIES

- 11 dark purple lilac stems
- 7 cream tulip stems
- 3 magenta waxflower sprays
- Clear pitcher or vase
- Floral tape
- Scissors
- Diagonal wire cutters
- Safety glasses

Make a lilac arrangement to welcome in the spring season.

NOTE

I chose dark purple lilacs for this arrangement for two reasons: I prefer the dark variety, and I found that the dark purple looked a little more convincing than the distinct light purple when I was shopping for the faux blooms for this arrangement. White lilacs could also be used for a monochromatic spring arrangement that would be so lovely and fresh.

Instructions

1. To start, you'll want to create a **frame** for your arrangement by placing clear floral tape across the mouth of your pitcher in a grid layout. More detailed instructions and photographs of this technique can be found on page 76. Although you could place your flowers directly into the vase and call it a day, the shape and polish of your arrangement greatly benefits from taking this first step.

2. For this design, I decided to forgo greenery and allow the lilacs to act as the **foundation** for the rest of the arrangement. I divided my lilacs into three piles—five stems would become the bottom layer, five stems would become the middle layer, and two stems would become the top layer.

3. Starting with the bottom layer, I removed all the extra leaves below the main bloom. (This may feel wrong, but trust me, the finished arrangement will look much better if the blooms have more room to breathe!) Then I used the wire cutters to trim the stems to size, so that when placed into the pitcher, the base of the bloom would rest on the mouth and spill out. When placing the bottom layer of stems, I visualized a pentagon over my tape grid, with the point of the pentagon lining up with the spout of my pitcher.

4. I placed the five stems in the outermost squares of my grid, at each point of the imaginary pentagon. So, while this finished arrangement looks loose and flowing, I used the idea of radial symmetry to make it.

5. Next, I moved to the top layer and cut 2 lilacs about 3"–4" (7.60–10.15cm) taller than the bottom layer. I faced the curved blooms toward each other so they met in the center and formed a "V" shape, and then inserted them both together into the centermost square of my grid.

6. I used my eye to judge how tall I wanted the arrangement and trimmed until I was happy with the look.

7. Now that I had the width and the height of my arrangement defined, I continued by filling in the gaps with my middle layer of lilacs. I trimmed and placed these stems as I went, about 1"–2" (2.55–5.10cm) longer than the bottom layer. I tried to place these stems equidistantly around the middle of the vase, offsetting these stems from the bottom layer so each bloom had its own "window."

8. Lilacs are line flowers (have many small buds growing up a center stalk instead of a single flower head), which makes them directional. I tried to pay attention to where the tops of the lilacs were pointing, placing stems at different angles to balance the arrangement and not have too many blooms pointing in the same direction.

9. While the lush lilacs are really the statement maker, I added cream tulips to create contrast and **focal** points around the arrangement. I tried to space these in a balanced way around the arrangement, removing the extra leaves and trimming them to size as I went. This part took a little bit of trial and error until I found placements for the tulips that looked like a natural fit with the lilacs. I also paid attention to the positioning of each tulip bloom, trying to vary the direction they faced and how open the petals were, to make them a little less perfect and more real.

10. For **filler** flowers, I chose magenta waxflowers to complement the dark purple lilacs. My waxflowers came in a spray, so I first cut down the spray into individual stems. Then I started placing the waxflowers into my arrangement, focusing on filling any empty spots and creating an even distribution of color throughout the arrangement as a whole.

11. Lastly, I turned the arrangement around on my lazy Susan, making adjustments and bending the lilac blooms slightly downward to give it a more relaxed feel. I used my fingers to open up some of the tulip blossoms just a bit.

ALTERNATE IDEA

Arrange your lilacs in a tall blue and white jar for a classic, colorful, and traditional look!

TIP
Always trim conservatively at the beginning, especially if you are using a clear vase. You can always trim more off as needed. Cut your stems at an angle and vary the lengths slightly for a more natural look.

"My favorite trick is to use a hair dryer for shaping faux flowers. It will smooth the material so you are able to shape how you want. If a flower is too open, for instance, you can close it up a bit by just heating it up and shaping it with your hands or leaving it inside of a small jar for a while."

—*Eveline Leake of The Macadamia Shop, Clifton Park, NY*

Pastel Peony and Eucalyptus Wreath

Peonies feel so quintessentially "spring" to me. They come in many beautiful colors and varieties, and I've found them to be one of the more convincing flowers for faux. They are a popular choice for wedding bouquets, and even look beautiful on their own in an arrangement or just a single bloom in a bud vase. I couldn't think of a better flower to welcome in the season with a beautiful spring wreath!

I chose peonies in tones of pale blush and peach for a pastel color scheme, with silvery lamb's ear and a couple different types of eucalyptus to add textural interest to this rather simple design. The result is a wreath that feels soft and fresh, even though it's faux! Place this on your front door for a boost to your curb appeal or display it indoors—it's beautiful either way.

SUPPLIES

- 2 large pink peony stems
- 2 medium pink peony stems with bud
- 8 silver dollar eucalyptus stems
- Gray-green mini eucalyptus bush
- 2 lamb's ear stems
- Additional greenery spray of your choice
- Wire wreath form
- Wire cutters
- Floral wire
- Safety glasses

This blush and pastel wreath feels fresh and pretty.

NOTE

There are many types of wreath forms you can use to get a similar look.
I created this wreath using with a wire wreath form. More detailed instructions and
photographs of this technique can be found on page 86.

Instructions

1. Start by prepping the **frame** of your wreath, in this case a wire wreath form. I laid my wreath form with the concave side facing up so my florals would nestle into this curve.

2. Pull your paddle wire out 1' (30.50cm) or so and attach it to the wreath form without cutting. I wrapped it around the middle two pieces of wire of my form using an "S" formation several times. Keep the wire attached to the paddle. You won't cut the wire until the end.

3. For the **foundation** of your wreath, create small bunches of your greenery to be wired to the wreath. Starting with the eucalyptus, break down the stems into small sprigs and arrange them in a pile. Break down the lamb's ear the same way you did the eucalyptus.

4. I decided I wanted my wreath to be mostly eucalyptus with a little lamb's ear sprinkled throughout for texture. I used about four to six sprigs per bundle and included lamb's ear in every other bundle so they would be evenly spaced out across the wreath. Follow the technique on page 86 for attaching bundles to the wreath form using paddle floral wire.

5. Continue until you have about two-thirds of the wreath covered in bunches.

6. In this wreath, the **focal** point is the peonies. After playing around with a few arrangements, I decided I wanted my wreath to feature two large peonies with smaller peony blooms and buds surrounding them.

7. To finish off my wreath, I made two more greenery bunches and placed one large peony, one medium peony, and one peony bud in each of them. When I wired them to the wreath, I did them in opposite directions so that one peony bunch tucked into the other. I placed the third medium-sized peony in between the two bunches, which helped to blend the transition between the two bundles.

8. Lastly, I filled in any sparse spots with more **filler** greenery, running a thin bead of hot glue to the stem before pushing it into the wreath.

Hanging Herb Garden

I think every room needs a bit of greenery, including the kitchen! I love the idea of using potted herbs as décor. The only trouble is that herbs can be tricky to grow indoors. A pot of basil may look perfect on the open shelving in your kitchen, but if it doesn't get the light it needs there, it won't grow well. Also, if you cut from and cook with herbs a lot, your herbs will probably always be looking a bit lopsided and scraggly.

Whether you have a green thumb or not, this is one example where I think it makes sense to mix in some faux. A hanging planter can fill an empty space between cabinets and add some visual interest at eye level, instead of having all your décor on your countertop. With this project idea, you have the feeling of fresh herbs in your kitchen all year round, and they'll be maintenance free.

SUPPLIES

- 2 terracotta pots of your choice
- Drill with various size masonry bits
- Large bucket
- Leather cording
- Floral foam
- Floral foam tools
- Rosemary bush
- Thyme bush
- Hot glue gun
- Dark brown craft paper (optional)

Using hanging faux herb plants in the kitchen will add fresh greenery to your kitchen without the high maintenance that comes with real herbs.

NOTE

I decided to make my own two-tier planter hung by leather cording because I wanted something unique! Feel free to customize the design however you like. Use twine or beaded macramé cord, paint your pots . . . the options are endless.

Instructions

1. The structure of this hanging planter is simple— two terracotta pots connected to each other and hung from leather cording. Before I drilled holes for the leather cording to loop through, the first thing I did was soak the pots in a bucket full of water for a good 24 hours. Terracotta can be drilled with a masonry bit, but to prevent the porous surface from cracking, it should be thoroughly soaked.

2. Once my pots were adequately soaked, I measured the circumference of the pot and marked the three places I wanted to drill holes. To drill, I started slowly with ¼" (0.65cm) bit, and then worked up to a ⅜" (0.95cm) bit to accommodate the width of my leather cording. Starting with the smallest bit and going up incrementally will decrease the risk of cracking your pot.

A simple, basic knot is all you need for this plant hanger.

The best part about creating
faux plant hangers is that you
don't have to worry about
making a watery mess.

3. Once the holes were drilled, I left the pots to dry for another 24 hours before assembling. I cut three lengths of leather cording, approximately 3' (91.45cm) each, and threaded them through the holes of the bottom pot, tying simple knots to secure the pots in place.

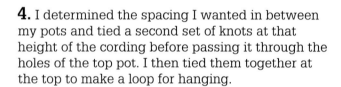

4. I determined the spacing I wanted in between my pots and tied a second set of knots at that height of the cording before passing it through the holes of the top pot. I then tied them together at the top to make a loop for hanging.

5. Next, I cut and hot-glued dry floral foam into each pot to create the base for my faux herbs. More detailed instructions and photographs of this technique can be found on page 80.

6. If your herbs are going to be hung at a height where you'll be able to see into them, you may want to disguise the foam. Moss is commonly used to hide floral foam, but you can also create convincing faux dirt using coffee grounds. For my project, I went with a no-mess version and just used brown textured scrapbooking paper cut into a ring that I slipped over the floral foam.

ALTERNATE
IDEA

If this project is a little too DIY-
heavy for you, feel free to use a
premade hanging planter or a
simple macramé plant hanger
such as this one!

CHAPTER 7:

SUMMER

Faux arrangements can be easy and exciting to make for the summer because of the wide variety of flora you can use. See pages 124–129 to see how I made this succulent garden.

Summer Meadow Flowers

For this arrangement, I found inspiration in two places. First, I attribute my vision for this project to the wildflower fields of Northern California, where poppies and lupines bloom every June and July. Nature truly does it best! I love the way the tall, columnar shape of the lupines complements the soft, crinkled petals of the poppies. Second, I found inspiration in fine art, specifically the still life work of 17th century Dutch painters like Rachel Ruysch. The dramatic shapes and vibrant colors of the flowers in her paintings are so striking. I wanted to bring a little bit of that artistic flair to my living room with this arrangement!

I went for nearly a full rainbow effect for the color scheme: red, orange, yellow, green, and blue. This arrangement can be recreated with a wide variety of faux flowers (parrot tulips and irises would be lovely!) and is beautiful displayed as an accent on a dresser or console table in your home.

SUPPLIES

- 3 large poppy stems in deep red, red orange, and white
- 2–3 medium poppy stems in yellow and orange
- 2 white buttercup stems
- Poppy pod stem
- 3 blue lupine sprays
- 5 large fern leaves
- Cascading greenery spray of your choice
- Floral foam
- Floral foam tools
- Pedestal vessel or urn

This rainbow arrangement can be recreated with any flowers you like.

NOTE

This asymmetrical arrangement has a definite front and back side, but you could place your greenery more symmetrically and add more florals to customize this project into a centerpiece that looks good from all directions.

Instructions

1. I used floral foam as the **frame** for this arrangement, but a similar look could be achieved with chicken wire (see page 78), a pin frog (see page 82), or a tape grid (see page 76). First, I cut the dry floral foam to size so the top of the foam would sit about 1" (2.55cm) higher than the mouth of the urn. I then trimmed the foam at a 45-degree angle all the way around the top to give myself more surface area for placing my florals.

2. Next, I created the **foundation** of my arrangement using my greenery (in this case, ferns). I placed five fern stems around the base of the arrangement, forming a "collar" that hid my floral foam. I chose to create a triangular shape for the structure of my arrangement, with ferns spreading wide on each side and a high point, just off-center at the top of my arrangement. I placed a spray cascading greenery in the lower right corner, but place your greenery where it looks best to you.

3. Instead of choosing one flower as my **focal** point, I decided to create a triangle center point with my three large poppies. I placed my red-orange poppy near the bottom of the arrangement, which also helped to hide the floral foam.

To create the focal point, my three largest poppies (the two red and one white) were placed in a triangular arrangement.

4. I arranged the white and dark red poppies at slightly different heights to further define the shape of my arrangement. Placing the poppies in a triangular shape helps to move the eye around the arrangement and balance the asymmetrical shape.

5. Once my focal flowers were in position, I began adding my **filler** flowers, starting from biggest to smallest. I placed my medium-size poppies in bunches of two and three to mimic the way flowers grow in clumps in nature.

6. With my three stems of blue lupines, I created a second triangle that was offset from the central triangle so that it filled out the arrangement more.

7. I cut apart the two poppy pods that came on one stem and placed them in the arrangement, one near the bottom and one near the top.

8. Finally, I filled in any empty areas with white buttercups. I love how the yellow-orange centers complement the poppies and fit with the wildflower theme.

"I'm very much guided by the shapes and lines of the flowers and branches I have to work with. Nature knows best, and I often find my designs flow easily—and end up looking best—when I try not to force the elements. My best advice would be to lean into it and go with the flow."

—*Anna Falkon of Gooseberry Hill Farm, Adelaide Hills, South Australia*

Feathery Fern and Wildflower Wreath

For this wreath design, I wanted to capture the feeling of a warm summer day. I have so many wonderful childhood memories of walking through the woods past the cornfields at our family farm, picking weeds and wildflowers for little bouquets with my sister, and eating wild raspberries right off the bushes that grew behind our grandmother's house.

I chose a grapevine wreath so it would look like the ferns and flowers were just growing out of the branches, the same way native plants sprout from between twigs and bark on the forest floor. I kept a pretty loose color scheme of blues, purples, yellows, white, raspberry red, and, of course, green. Something about summer makes all the colors of the rainbow come alive! This wreath would make a beautiful statement on your front door or hung on the wall of a screened-in porch or covered patio to enjoy all summer long.

SUPPLIES

- 2 fern bushes
- 2 blue-purple waxflower sprays
- 2 feverfew daisy sprays
- 2 blue cornflower sprays
- Yellow yarrow spray
- Red raspberry bush
- Hot glue gun
- Grapevine wreath
- All-purpose floral wire
- Wire cutters

Allowing a grapevine wreath to show through your faux flowers gives your finished piece an earthy look.

NOTE

Use a little hot glue at the end of each stem before placing it into the grapevine wreath. You want to push the stem snugly between the grapevine branches, but the addition of hot glue will give your florals just a little more security. Don't worry if you mess up; it's not hard to pull out a stem and try placing it again. But remember, it doesn't have to be perfect to be beautiful!

Instructions

1. First, I prepped my grapevine wreath, which is the **frame** of this design. I removed the tag (mine had a metal clamp that I had to cut to remove), tucked in any majorly loose branches, and secured some branches with glue or wire where necessary. Part of the charm of a grapevine wreath is its asymmetrical shape and wild branches, but you want to make sure it's structurally sound before you start assembling your wreath.

2. Before I started placing my florals, I attached a length of medium-gauge, all-purpose floral wire to the back of my wreath that I could use to hang it from.

3. I chose ferns as the **foundation** for my design. I cut down the fern bushes into individual fronds, leaving about 3" (7.60cm) of wire at the base. Next, I ran a thin bead of glue on the bottom of each stem and then tucked it into the grapevine wreath, pushing it between the branches for a snug fit. I started by placing ferns around the outside of the wreath, all in the same direction.

4. I went around a second time, placing fronds closer to the inside of the wreath. You can decide how loose or structured you want the wreath to be. I was going for a wild-meadow look, so I chose to let the ends of my ferns fall freely. If you want something a little more structured, you can place a dab of glue about three-quarters of the way up your fern frond to attach it back to the grapevine wreath.

5. For this wreath, I wanted more of an all-over texture than a set **focal** point, so I didn't use any large blooms. Instead, I mixed medium and small flowers throughout the wreath as both my focal and **filler** flowers. I cut all of my flower stems, sprays, and bushes down into smaller pieces, about 5"–6" (12.70–15.25cm) in length, including leaving some wire at the base to insert into the wreath form.

6. I chose a starting point on the wreath and began placing my florals. I began with the three yellow yarrow blossoms, placing them evenly around the wreath. Next, I added purple waxflower and feverfew daisies.

7. When I placed my six blue cornflowers, I varied the depth and where the blooms faced on the wreath. I tucked one straight on, placed others at an angle toward the inside of the wreath, and then angled others out toward the outside of the wreath.

8. After the cornflower, I placed my six raspberry bunches.

9. In addition to the berry bunches, I also pulled additional leaves off the raspberry bush and hot-glued them in between ferns around the wreath to add another texture to the greenery foundation of the wreath.

10. Lastly, I went back in and added more daisies, this time cutting the stems a bit longer so they would fill in some of the spaces between the outer tips of the fern fronds.

Birdcage Succulent Garden

Succulents are such a great option for crafting. With their waxy leaves and stems, their faux counterparts look very realistic! I wanted to get creative with an old birdcage that was gathering dust in my décor closet (yes, I have one of those!) that I knew I could repurpose.

Funny story about this birdcage: it was given to me as a birthday gift by my husband (then boyfriend) in 2011, when birdcages were quite a popular home décor object. He presented it to me with a vase of fresh cut flowers tucked inside and we were both impressed with his creativity. Birdcages have fallen a bit out of fashion—as trendy décor tends to do—but I knew with a fresh coat of paint, I could modernize and reimagine it as a succulent garden. This project would look great hanging in a corner of your room, on a plant stand, or set on a dresser or tabletop.

SUPPLIES

- 4–6 large succulent picks
- 2–3 mini/clustering succulent picks
- 2 tall succulent picks
- 3 trailing succulent sprays
- 8" (20.30cm) dome dry floral foam
- Moss
- Greening pins
- Hot glue gun
- Birdcage with removable base

Faux succulents can easily be mistaken for real plants.

NOTE

To recreate this project, you'll want to find a birdcage that has a fully removable bottom. That way you'll be able to glue your dry floral foam to the base and then reassemble partway through inserting your succulents to ensure it all fits back together!

Instructions

1. First, I removed the base from my birdcage and hot-glued the foam onto it.

2. I added a layer of moss around the base using greening pins. I knew the middle and top of my foam would be mostly covered in succulents, so I left that part bare, keeping in mind that I could fill in with more moss later if necessary.

3. I worked on establishing the shape of my succulent arrangement, starting with the high point. I placed my two tallest succulent picks toward the top of the dome shape but slightly staggered and off-center for a more natural look.

4. I knew I wanted my low point to be a collection of trailing succulents (faux string of pearls sprays) focused toward the lower right side, but I decided to place those last after I had reassembled the birdcage.

5. I placed the other larger succulents toward the top and middle of the dome, alternating colors and shapes in the arrangement in the way that looked best to me.

6. I carefully reassembled the birdcage, then began filling in with my smaller, clustered succulents by pushing them in between the wires of the birdcage and into the foam. I placed two stems of trailing succulents in the lower right side and one on the left side a little further back, threading the pieces through the wire of the birdcage to make it look like they had grown that way.

7. Anywhere I could still see the floral foam showing through, I filled with moss. Then I disguised the greening pins by hot-gluing a little clump of moss on top.

I waited to add the trailing
succulent plants until the end after
I reassembled the birdcage.

Pulling some of the succulents between the bars of the cage made this arrangement look like they naturally grew that way.

"An arrangement can have more interest and a modern touch if you go beyond the traditional globe shape."

—*Stephanie Petrak of Lorraine's Cottage, Cleveland, OH*

CHAPTER 8:
FALL

Fall is such a fun season when
it comes to décor, with all of the
reds, oranges, and browns.

Autumnal Fruit and Foliage

Fall has always been my favorite season, and this centerpiece has become one of my favorites as well! Instead of a vase, I used a vintage silver trophy that I found in a thrift store. There are so many creative ways to repurpose thrift-store or second-hand items in craft projects. Not only are you saving discarded items from going to the landfill, but incorporating found objects always gives a design more soul.

In keeping with the unique vessel, I tried to choose floral elements that were a bit uncommon, such as cream geraniums, black skimmia berries, plum branches, speckled euonymus branches, and miniature red-orange leaves. Using unexpected elements such as fruit, vegetables, berries, and branches is a great way to add texture and dimension to your designs.

SUPPLIES

- 4 cream geranium sprays
- 3 black skimmia berry stems
- 3 plum branches
- Euonymus leaf branch
- Red leafy branch
- Trophy or silver bowl
- Floral foam
- Floral foam tools
- Moss
- Greening pins
- Hot glue gun

I repurposed a vintage silver trophy I found at a thrift store, which mixes perfectly with the unique flower combination in this arrangement.

NOTE

For this project, I chose plum branches and black skimmia berries.
If you wanted something different, faux apples and cabbage, pears and pussy
willow branches, or citrus and hypericum berries would also be great combinations!

Instructions

1. First, I prepared the **frame** of my arrangement by cutting dry floral foam to size and securing it to the bottom of the trophy with hot glue. Because the diameter of the trophy was so wide, I had to use several pieces of floral foam pieced together to fill it.

2. I covered the foam with moss using greening pins.

3. Next, I started placing my greens, which are the **foundation** of this design. I placed one plum branch on either side to establish the width of my arrangement. Then I inserted my speckled euonymus leaf branch just off-center and pointing straight up to define the tallest point. I placed my third plum branch just down from the euonymus branch, angling outward.

4. For my **focal** point, I tried something a little bit different and clustered most of my cream geraniums off to one side, forming a subtle "C" shape. I cut each spray down into individual blooms so I would have more flexibility in placing them.

5. I created a bit of breathing room by placing my final geranium bloom on the opposite side, near the rim of the trophy. This asymmetrical placement creates some movement in the design.

"Don't be afraid to really bend and fluff the faux florals. This easily elevates your design by giving it a more natural look."
—*Stephanie Petrak of Lorraine's Cottage, Cleveland, OH*

The plum branches add interest to the arrangement without overwhelming the design.

The white geraniums are the focal point of this arrangement.

I chose black skimmia berries and red leaves as the fillers, which really help the geraniums stand out.

6. My **fillers** were black skimmia and red leaves. I started with the skimmia first, focusing their placement where there were holes or gaps in the arrangement.

7. For the red leaves, I cut the branch into two so I could form it around the single geranium bloom. I love the way the cream geranium, black skimmia, and red leaves contrast with the greenery.

When decorating your fall table with a colorful arrangement like this, keep your colors and patterns simple.

Dahlia Gold Hoop Wreath

Dahlias are one of my favorite flowers, and in the garden they usually bloom until September or October. The rich colors and textures of these flowers make them the perfect choice for fall in my mind.

I mixed tones of deep burgundy with mauve and a brighter coral for a varied, monochromatic color scheme. I chose to contrast the fullness of the dahlias with a minimalist gold hoop as the base of my wreath. I've admired this style of wreath for a while, and it was so fun to make my own! These simple wreaths look just as good hung indoors as wall art as they do on your front door.

SUPPLIES

- Large burgundy dahlia stem
- 2 medium dahlia sprays in mauve and coral
- Ficus branch
- Spiked fern spray
- 14" (35.55cm) gold metal hoop
- Floral stem tape in brown or green
- Fishing line

This wreath is a good example of a monochromatic color scheme.

NOTE

There are several different methods you can use for affixing your florals to your hoop.
I used floral stem tape, but I would recommend using all-purpose floral wire if you plan
to hang your wreath outside where it will be exposed to the elements.

Instructions

1. To start, I cut down the ficus branch into smaller pieces, and then laid them across the brass hoop to get an idea of how far I wanted the greenery **frame** of this wreath to spread.

2. I cut down the spiked fern spray to put with the ficus as a **filler** and to add texture to the wreath design.

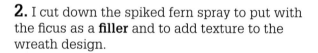

3. I organized the greenery pieces into two large bunches, securing the stems together by tightly wrapping them in floral stem tape.

4. Pointing each bunch in opposite directions, I secured them to the hoop. I made sure to leave some empty space in between for my florals.

5. The **focal** point of my wreath is the large burgundy dahlia. I cut down the stem to about 3" (7.60cm) in length and then bent it. This secured the stem to the center point of my wreath with the flower head facing forward.

6. I cut down my medium dahlia sprays into individual blooms and buds. I placed one mauve bloom with a coral bud to create one bunch, and one coral bloom with a mauve bud to make the second bunch.

7. Attach the side bunches to either side of the large burgundy dahlia, overlapping the greenery frame.

8. To hang, I added fishing line just off-center on the top of the wreath to counterbalance the weight of the flowers.

I love the contrast between the simple gold hoop and the large arrangement of flowers and greenery.

Marigold and Butterfly Cloche

From time to time, I've come across dried floral arrangements preserved in glass cloches in my vintage and antique shopping. I've always thought it was such a pretty way to display florals.

For this project, I applied the technique to faux. I wanted this design to feel like a little bit of nature captured in a jar, so I chose marigolds (which have significance for the fall celebration of Dia de los Muertos), Queen Anne's lace, brown curly willow branches, and dainty fabric butterflies (which I sourced from online).

Something about this project just feels so sweet and sentimental to me, like bottling up a fleeting moment in time. I displayed it in my daughter's nursery, but this project would make a lovely addition as décor on a bookshelf, mantle, or tabletop in any room.

SUPPLIES

- Curly willow branch
- Marigold spray
- 2 Queen Anne's lace sprays
- 2 fabric butterflies (optional)
- Floral pin frog
- Floral clay
- Cloche with base

I love the vintage look this glass cloche adds to this simple arrangement.

NOTE

I used a floral pin frog to secure my stems, and I also chose to leave the mechanics
of my arrangement exposed because I like the way the industrial pin frog contrasts
with the dainty florals. If you prefer, you can use dry floral foam instead and hide your
mechanics with moss or leaves for a more naturalistic look.

Instructions

1. To create the **frame** of this project, I affixed a pin frog to the base of the cloche with floral clay, making sure it was centered and secure. More detailed instructions and photographs of this technique can be found on page 82.

2. The **foundation** of this design is the Queen Anne's lace. I cut down the two sprays to slightly different heights and inserted them into the pin frog. This creates a staggered effect that fills the cylindrical shape of the cloche.

3. I chose marigolds as the **focal** flower and cut down the sprays into individual blooms of different heights. I placed three blooms in a triangular shape. The tallest was just a bit shorter than the height of the cloche, the shortest was just over half the height of the cloche, and the middle stem fell somewhere in between.

I wanted a staggered look to the overall arrangement, so I cut all the sprays to different lengths. This also gave my marigolds a triangular shape, which lends movement to the piece.

4. For **filler**, I used curly willow branches. I cut down the branch into smaller pieces. I made sure the branches were a bit taller than the height of the cloche so they would bend around the curved glass and form an interesting shape. I placed the taller stem in the back and the two shorter pieces of curly willow toward the front of the arrangement, training the flexible branches around the flowers until I found a placement I liked.

5. Adding two fabric butterflies gave the arrangement a touch of whimsy. I bent the wings a bit to make them look like they had perched for a moment mid-flight and secured them in place with a dab of hot glue.

6. As a final touch, I put the cloche onto the base, letting the curly willow branches bend to fit the shape.

I added a couple of
fabric butterflies to
give the arrangement a
little playfulness.

CHAPTER 9:
WINTER

Even though winter is not known for flowers, that doesn't mean that you can't use them in your arrangements.

Holiday Rose and Hellebore Centerpiece

With winter comes a season full of holiday celebrations. For the project, I was inspired to make a more traditional centerpiece for a dining table. I chose pine branches, glossy deep green ruscus, delicate red berries, and off-white Sophia roses and rose buds, all of which juxtaposed with a newfound favorite, hellebores.

Hellebores (also known as Christmas or Lenten roses) come in several varieties that bloom from winter to early spring. Their unique color and shapely stems provide great contrast to the more formal roses for a holiday arrangement that isn't your typical red and green. For the vessel, I removed the lid from a thrift-store ceramic soup tureen.

SUPPLIES

- 8 cream Sophia roses
- 7 cream rose buds
- 4 hellebore sprays
- Red berry spray
- Pine branch
- Ruscus branch
- Chicken wire
- Wire cutters
- Protective gloves
- Vintage ceramic soup tureen

Though this arrangement isn't your traditional red-and-green holiday arrangement, the pine branches and red berries still give it a wintery feel.

NOTE

For centerpieces like this one, it's especially helpful to use a lazy Susan.
That way you'll be able to turn your arrangement 360 degrees as you go,
making sure your finished design is beautiful from all angles.

Instructions

1. For the **frame** of this arrangement, I used chicken wire to form a ball inside the base of the soup tureen. More detailed instructions and photographs of this technique can be found on page 78.

2. The **foundation** greenery I used was pine and ruscus. I started with the pine, cutting down the branch into short pieces and placing them around the outside of the vessel—one at each corner. Then I placed two pine branches closer toward the center of the chicken wire, coming out at an angle.

3. I then did the same with the ruscus, placing four branches around the perimeter of the vessel and another couple toward the middle.

The off-white shade of these roses look so lovely when placed amongst the greenery and hellebores.

4. Next, I placed my **focal** flowers, cream Sophia roses and green hellebore tinged with red. I started with the roses, placing them in between the greenery evenly around the arrangement.

5. I placed my hellebore sprays in the gaps, inserting one toward the front of the arrangement near the rim of the tureen, one on either side at slightly different angles, and one in the back angling up so you could see it from the front. Really, this arrangement doesn't have a front or back, but for illustrative purposes I'm describing it the way it's shown here.

6. For **filler**, I first placed cream rosebuds in bunches of two and three in the empty spots between the roses, hellebore, and greenery.

7. Lastly, I accented with a few springs of red berry branches spread evenly throughout the arrangement. This little bit of texture and color draws out the red of the hellebore and provides contrast with the cream roses.

I like that the leafy ruscus doesn't look like the traditional evergreen plant, but it is something you could find outside on a cold, wintery day.

The difference in the hellebore and roses really come together in the end when all the other added elements are put in place.

Frosty Thistle and Juniper Wreath

This wreath was inspired by the colors and textures found in nature during the winter season. Even though I used faux, I wanted the wreath to look foraged—like I could have found all the greens on a snowy walk through the woods.

I started with a grapevine wreath as my base, but lightly coated in a chalky white spray paint so it has the look of being dusted with snow. Instead of covering the whole wreath, I focused my botanical elements on the upper left quadrant, leaving a good bit of the wreath form exposed. I love this style of wreath for a simple, rustic feel. I chose pine, juniper with blue-gray berries, broadleaf eucalyptus, and blue thistle for an analogous color scheme of blues and greens. The finishing touches were a pair of silver jingle bells and a green bow to add some subtle holiday cheer!

SUPPLIES

- Juniper branch with berries
- Pine branch
- Broadleaf eucalyptus spray
- 2 blue thistle sprays
- Grapevine wreath
- White spray paint in chalky finish
- 2 silver jingle bells
- Ribbon of your choice
- Hot glue gun

This rustic wreath is made by combining a blue-green color scheme and an exposed white grapevine wreath.

NOTE

You can customize this wreath to whatever wintery color scheme you like best.
For an earthy, traditional color scheme, simply swap the thistle for red berries,
the silver bells for flocked pinecones, and the green bow for white ribbon.

Instructions

1. First, I prepped my grapevine wreath, which is the **frame** of this design. I removed the tag (mine had a metal clamp that I had to cut to remove), tucked in any majorly loose branches, and secured with glue or wire where necessary.

2. To give the grapevine branches a wintery touch, I sprayed the wreath form with two very light coats of white chalk paint. Once it was fully dry, I attached a length of medium-gauge, all-purpose floral wire to the back of my wreath that I could use to hang it from.

3. Before placing my **foundation** of greenery, I chose the central point on the wreath where my branches would emanate from. Starting with the pine, I placed one branch on either side of this center point in opposite directions with the ends pointing out. Just like in the Feathery Fern and Wildflower Wreath (see page 120), I dipped the bottom of the stems in hot glue before pushing them in between the vines to secure.

4. I placed a third, shorter pine branch pointing up at an angle from my central point, and then continued placing pine branches until I was happy with the look. I wanted the juniper branches to be more visible, which is why I placed them on top of the pine.

5. I followed the same steps, alternating branches toward the outside edge and the inside edge of the wreath to get the fullness I wanted.

6. Next, I started on the **focal** point of my wreath. First, I cut my thistle sprays down into individual stems, and then placed three on either side of the central point.

7. I used all-purpose floral wire to string my silver jingle bells together and attach them to the wreath. I pulled the ends of the wire through the grapevine branches and to the back of the wreath, twisting to secure. I tied a bow out of simple, green cotton ribbon and used a dab of hot glue to attach it just above the bells.

8. To finish off this design, I added a few sprigs of broadleaf eucalyptus as a **filler**. I really liked the way the shape of the leaves contrasted the evergreen branches and the how blue-green color aligns with the blue of the thistle blossoms.

Magnolia and Boxwood Garland

A lush, green garland draped over a staircase bannister is my very favorite winter decoration. Fresh pine garland needs to be misted with water frequently to keep it alive, and even then, one garland will probably not last more than two weeks.

For a beautiful display that will last all season long, I think faux greenery is the best choice. Plus, you only need to buy the materials for a faux garland once and then you can reuse it year after year!

I wanted to create a simple evergreen garland with a mixture of natural textures that could serve as an elegant base to a variety of florals and decorations. I used a combination of inexpensive pine garland layered with premade boxwood garland and cedar branches. At the top of each swag, I accented with a pair of large white magnolia flowers to finish out my project.

SUPPLIES
- 6 lengths of pine garland
- 3 premade boxwood garlands
- 6 magnolia stems
- 3 cedar branches
- Box of garland ties

The large magnolia blooms are an excellent way to add some interest.

NOTE

If you wanted to fancy-up this garland for a holiday party, it would look lovely with large
bows hung below the magnolia flowers, or with glass ball ornaments strung among the branches.
And, of course, strands of warm white lights will always spread holiday cheer!

Instructions

1. To start, I took two basic pine garlands and loosely twisted them together for more fullness. Every 1' (30.50cm) or so, I secured two of the wired branches together to connect the two garlands.

2. Next, I added reusable garland ties. They work in a similar way to nylon cable ties but are clear silicone to blend with their background. It's helpful to hang the garland on the banister at this step. I chose to do two swags along the railing and then wrap the newel post, letting the garland drape down to the floor. I went back and fluffed the pine branches individually, straightening the wired branches and adjusting them to various angles.

By combining faux pine, boxwood, and cedar, this trailing banister garland looks full and perfectly textured.

I varied the direction in which the magnolias were facing so they didn't look too structured.

3. Next, I took my premade boxwood garlands and layered them on top of the pine garlands, using the wire ends to tie them in. I adjusted the stems of the pines again around the boxwood so they would overlap and fit together naturally.

4. After that, I cut down my magnolia stems to about 6" (15.25cm) and bent the stem back so it made a right angle with the flower head. At each swag of the garland, I pushed two magnolia blossoms into the pine garland base, varying the direction each bloom was facing for more dimension.

5. Lastly, I inserted cedar branches in around the magnolia for a contrast of texture and color. Because I was starting with a base of the wired pine garland, I didn't need to use any other wire or glue to fasten my floral elements for this project. It really couldn't be simpler to put together! No wires or adhesives mean it will be just as easy to disassemble and store at the end of the season.

I let the garland drape down to the floor so it doesn't look as restrained as it would if I'd wrapped the whole post.

This garland was attached to the banister without glue or wires to make it easy to move when the holidays are over.

Inspiration Gallery

Creating faux flower décor is very personal, and the look you achieve with your pieces depends entirely on your preferences for color and design. When brainstorming new ideas, however, it's always helpful to look to what other crafters and florists have done to find the direction you want to go in. This gallery here will provide a few tips and inspiration from me to you. My hope is that you fall in love with faux floral crafting, and are able to create pieces for your own home that speak to you.

For an elegant holiday table, work with muted colors in your centerpiece.

There are so many different types of faux greenery plants available in stores. Your choice depends on the look you're trying to achieve.

Faux table centerpieces for a party are great because you can prepare them ahead of time, before the mayhem of planning really starts.

This arrangement doesn't have much greenery, which allows the vibrant lilacs to take center stage.

Use unexpected vessels when creating your faux plant pieces.

Create pieces for the room you plan to place them in, like how this colorful arrangement works really well in this dark room.

Get a little extra crafty and create some macramé hangers for your faux planters.

For a unique and interesting arrangement, consider using found or thrifted items and vessels, such as this birdcage I'd had for years before putting it to better use.

When choosing monochromatic color schemes, use multiple hues within the scheme to keep your piece from looking dull.

Instead of using a floral centerpiece or fabric table runner, why not create a gorgeous garland instead?

You can always find filler flowers with more than one pop of color that will work to help bring unity to your piece.

If you love the look of hanging planters, but don't have the time, patience, or lighting to deal with real plants, go faux!

Resources

Quality faux flowers, botanicals, and greenery and supplies can be found at your local craft stores and independent retailers, as well as through many online retailers. I've put together this quick list of my favorite resources for purchasing these items.

Afloral

www.Afloral.com

Afloral sells high-quality and affordable silk flowers and floral décor. You can use its products to create pieces for your home or a special occasion. A section of its website is dedicated to DIY tips and videos. In addition to faux florals, Afloral sells dried flowers, live plants, vases, and supplies.

Crate & Barrel

www.CrateandBarrel.com

Crate & Barrel is a home décor retailer. It sells ready-made faux planters, wreaths, and garlands, as well as stems, sprays, and bunches of a variety of plants. Crate & Barrel also sells a host of unique and stylish vases.

FloraCraft

www.FloraCraft.com

FloraCraft is an eco-friendly, family-owned manufacturer of craft foam products, as well as floral tools and accessories. Its products are available to purchase through many online and in-store retailers.

Flower & Home Marketplace

www.FlowerandHome.com

Flower & Home Marketplace is a home décor retailer that sells floral products for your home, as well as other decorative products. Its floral products include everything from stems to pick and wreaths to garlands.

Jamali Garden

www.JamaliGarden.com

Jamali Garden is a wholesale retailer for anyone who works with flowers, from florists to set designers. It sells home and party décor as well as floral supplies. Its silk flowers and plants include individual sprays and picks and potted artificial plants.

Magnolia

https://shop.Magnolia.com

Magnolia is the company run by HGTV's *Fixer Upper* stars, Joanna and Chip Gaines. In addition to the rustic décor the Magnolia brand is known for, it sells loose faux flowers and greenery. A variety of vessels, wreaths, and ready-made faux floral décor are also sold.

Pottery Barn

www.PotteryBarn.com

Pottery Barn specializes in selling a whole host of products and furniture pieces for the home, including potted and arranged artificial flowers and plants. If you want to create your own pieces, Pottery Barn also sells loose faux botanicals, vases, planters, and pots.

Save on Crafts

www.Save-on-Crafts.com

Save on Crafts sells affordable, high-quality products for weddings, parties, homes, and DIY projects. In addition to faux florals and greenery, they carry a variety of vases, floral supplies, and planters.

Terrain

www.shopTerrain.com

Terrain is a modern home décor retailer that sells everything you might need to decorate your home. Among its products, it sells a large assortment of fresh, dried, and faux plant stems, sprays, and branches.

West Elm

www.westelm.com

west elm is a branch of Williams-Sonoma, Inc. that sells affordable, modern pieces for the home. In addition to bath, bedding, and outdoor products, it sells faux flowers and greenery, as well as a bunch of interesting, chic vases and planters.

Faux botanicals are readily available at local retailers and online. The hardest part will be choosing which flowers to buy!

Index

Note: Page numbers in *italics* indicate projects.

Acknowledgments

First, I would like to thank the team at Fox Chapel Publishing, my amazing photographer, Savannah Smith, and also my sponsors, Afloral and FloraCraft, for making this book possible. I would also like to thank the florists and makers who so generously shared their passion and knowledge with me: Meghan Conners, Shea Mack, LaParis Phillips, Eveline Leake, Anna Falkon, Stephanie Kirby, Alyssa Grogan, and Stephanie Petrak. Most of all, I would like to thank my family and friends for their unfailing support and encouragement, especially Frankie Greek, Jessica Weikert, and my husband, Anthony Storck, who were my personal book advisory team. I couldn't have written this book without their help. And last but not least, I'd like to thank my daughter, Sage, who is my inspiration in all things. The idea for this book was born into the world just a couple months after she was.

Credits

Supplies for this book were sponsored in part by Afloral® and FloraCraft.

All images in this book were captured by Savannah Smith Photography unless otherwise noted.

Image on page 28 by SC Stockshop (*www.SCStockshop.com*).

Decorative illustrations throughout as follows: The Pen and Brush/Creative Market (jacket spine, 7, 8 bottom, 10); Freepik.com (4, 8 top, 9, 14, 18, 20, 28, 30, 36, 42, 48, 52, 54, 60, 69, 70, 72, 77, 81, 85, 92, 100, 166, 170, 172, 176); Irikul/Freepik.com (12, 33, 39, 45, 52, 92)

About the Author

Stevie Storck is a professional interior designer, writer, and creative entrepreneur. The inspiration she found in the spaces we live, work, play, and dream led her to study Interior Architecture at Chatham University, where she earned her bachelor's degree in 2013. Three years later, she opened Stevie Storck Design Co. and has been serving residential design clients in Pennsylvania and beyond ever since. Stevie's work focuses on the powerful connection between our outer environment and our inner peace, happiness and contentment. She is passionate about creating thoughtfully designed interiors that are as beautiful, unique, and soulful as the people they are designed for.

In addition to interior design, Stevie has been writing about crafts, DIY projects, simple homemaking, and intentional living since she started her first blog nearly ten years ago. Stevie's writing has been published on the *Huffington Post*, and she has been featured for her design skills in *Susquehanna Style Magazine, LNP | Lancaster Online*, and more. Stevie resides in York County, Pennsylvania, with her husband, Anthony, and their daughter, Sage.